THE UNIVERSITY:
INTERNATIONAL EXPECTATION

The University

International Expectations

Edited by
F. KING ALEXANDER
and
KERN ALEXANDER

McGill-Queen's University Press
Montreal & Kingston · London · Ithaca

ISBN 0-7735-2248-4 (cloth)
ISBN 0-7735-2249-2 (paper)

Legal deposit fourth quarter 2002
Bibliothèque nationale du Québec

Printed in Canada on acid-free paper that is 100% ancient forest free
(100% post-consumer recycled), processed chlorine free.

This book has been published with the help of a grant from the
Oxford Round Table, which meets at St Anthony's College, Oxford,
England, with American headquarters at Godstow Hall, 2837 Riedling
Drive, Louisville, Kentucky 40206.

McGill-Queen's University Press acknowledges the support of the
Canada Council for the Arts for its publishing program. It also
acknowledges the financial support of the Government of Canada
through the Book Publishing Industry Development Program (BPIDP)
for its publishing activities.

National Library of Canada Cataloguing in Publication

Main entry under title:
The university: international expectations / edited by F. King Alexander and
Kern Alexander.
Includes bibliographical references and index.
ISBN 0-7735-2448-4 (bound) –
ISBN 0-7735-2249-2 (pbk.)
1. Education, Higher. 2. Education, Higher – Aims and objectives.
I. Alexander, Kern II. Alexander, F. King
LB2322.2.U56 2002   378   C2002-901922-2

Typeset in Palatino 10/13
by Caractéra inc., Quebec City

FOR ELIZABETH

Contents

Preface

The University: International Expectations provides discussion of prevailing issues and expectations that confront college and university leaders on four continents. The reader will quickly see that the global environment in which higher education functions today poses complex questions that education leaders must resolve if their initiatives are to succeed. While the book deals with colleges and universities only in the English-speaking countries of Australia, Canada, South Africa, the United Kingdom, and the United States, the issues raised are relevant for other countries that have relatively well-developed systems of higher education. The book moves from the general to the specific, with the introductory chapter (by Kern Alexander) presenting the ever-perplexing dilemma of the "what and why" of university existence, the object of the enterprise, and its relationship to a particular state and nation. Should the university inform the state or should the state prescribe the purpose of the university? Questions regarding university autonomy and freedom to create its own design are implicit in all aspects of this question. Much of the book is devoted to a discussion of measures needed to overcome inertia in universities and the need for responsiveness to the social and economic changes that permeate university cultures. Constantly "reinventing" the university (see Don Aitkin's chapter on Australia's experience) as a relevant part of society and facilitating the adaptations needed to maintain it as a critical mechanism in social progress are of central importance to higher education, regardless of the nature of the government under which it operates.

Within this broad agenda, the book raises questions that can be most clearly addressed within the context of existing national systems of higher education. Ontario's experience with regard to centralization of decision-making and the efficacies of alternative organizational structures (see Ian Clark's chapter) is informative for federal systems that support higher education, particularly Australia and the United States. Questions of the efficiency and effectiveness of the delivery of educational services and the university's responsiveness to both the taxpayer and the student are of paramount concern throughout the book. Universities operate under the constraints of the public's expectations, requiring maximization of resources. The search for higher levels of performance and greater quality and quantity of higher education at ever lesser costs intensifies with every passing decade. In this regard, one chapter (by F. King Alexander) in particular highlights performance requirements in the United Kingdom and the United States, forming interesting parallels and demonstrating strengths and weaknesses that should be of considerable interest to practising university leaders and legislators alike.

Two chapters are devoted to different aspects of human rights that are directly and appropriately of concern to universities. The ability of the university to aid in advancing the state of human rights may constitute its greatest test. The situation in South Africa (see David R. Woods) is in the forefront of this discussion as institutions of higher education in that country seek to redress the pervasive social and economic misdeeds of the past. Moreover, the legal difficulties involved in the quest for human rights in Europe and the United States are presented in some detail (by Michael J. Beloff); the adaptation of England and Wales to the standards of the European Convention on Human Rights is highlighted.

The book also addresses the vital question of how to deal with increasing costs, as well as the issue of public versus private institutional competition (John H. Moore) and the emergence of the private for-profit institution as a rising player in post-secondary education, particularly in the United States (Stephen R. Greenwald). As observed herein, the challenge that proprietary educational corporations pose for traditional private non-profit institutions will not be easily or quickly resolved.

Finally, two chapters of the book are devoted to the phenomenon of technology and information flow that is altering the traditional structure of the university. The legal implications of internet use and the risks to universities created by foreign legal jurisdictions are discussed (by James J. Mingle), as are the realities of how technology can be used to improve college and university instruction and the overall experience of higher education (David W. Olien).

All the chapters are written by university leaders who are actively involved in dealing with the matters involved. The problems raised do not have simple solutions, but we hope that the insights provided about options and alternatives will make this a valuable book for people in leadership positions in colleges and universities.

We are greatly indebted to friends and colleagues who rendered timely and valuable service in the production of this book. Of singular importance to the project was the work of Shenette Campbell, who so ably coordinates and facilitates the annual conduct of the Oxford Round Table. Manuscript production was in the hands of Bridgette Garrison, who, as always, turned out a quality product with alacrity and Dr. Klint Alexander, who proofed and critiqued the manuscript. Our efforts were greatly facilitated by Shirley Fryer and Diana Whitt of the University of Illinois, Urbana-Champaign, both of whom were indispensable players in all aspects of our endeavours. Particular recognition must be extended to Dr. Kathe Kasten, dean of the College of Education and Human Services, University of North Florida, Jacksonville, who provided a congenial academic environment in which to study and write. During the past year the editors were academic itinerants, moving in and about three fine universities. Given this, we acknowledge with profound appreciation the goodwill and support of our dear friends at Murray State University, who provided us with the home for which we are thankful – and on which we are highly dependent. Finally, we thank John Parry, Kyla Madden, and Joan McGilvray of McGill-Queen's University Press, who provided exemplary professional assistance in the final development and publication of this book.

FKA   Urbana-Champaign, Illinois
KA   Jacksonville, Florida

Contributors

DON AITKIN is vice-chancellor and professor of the University of Canberra, Australia.

F. KING ALEXANDER was formerly director of the Higher Education Administration Program and assistant professor, College of Education and the Institute of Government and Public Affairs (IGPA), University of Illinois at Champaign. He now serves as president of Murray State University in Kentucky.

KERN ALEXANDER is director of the Oxford Round Table. He also holds the Andrew Robinson Eminent Scholar Chair at the University of North Florida and is professor of education administration in the University of Illinois at Champaign.

MICHAEL J. BELOFF is president of Trinity College, Oxford. He serves as judge of the Court of Appeal of Jersey and Guernsey, member of the Court of Arbitration for Sport, and deputy chairman, Data Protection Tribunal for National Security Matters, United Kingdom.

IAN CLARK is president of the Council of Ontario Universities, Canada.

STEPHEN R. GREENWALD is president of Audrey Cohen College in New York.

JAMES J. MINGLE is university counsel and secretary of the corporation at Cornell University in Ithaca, New York.

JOHN H. MOORE is president of Grove City College in Pennsylvania.

DAVID W. OLIEN is senior vice-president for administration in the University of Wisconsin System at Madison.

DAVID R. WOODS, a former Rhodes scholar, is president of Rhodes University in Grahamstown, South Africa.

THE UNIVERSITY:
INTERNATIONAL EXPECTATIONS

The Object of the University: Motives and Motivation

KERN ALEXANDER

The intention in this paper is not to delve into the recesses of the idea of the university as conceived by John Henry Newman[1] or Jaroslav Pelikan,[2] but rather to discuss the university is relation to government, its objectives, and its role in society. The question is an important one and should be addressed, implicitly or explicitly, by universities, states, and nations. One could say simply, that the quest of the university is for an educated citizenry – probably the essence of the issue. Yet consideration of the issue has historically produced several and varied responses, most of them insightful and worthy in their own contexts. This paper is meant to contribute some thoughts to the discussion and to observe that simplicity and certainty in answers to the question are elusive indeed.

To define specifically the object of the university and to enunciate motives and motivation assume that such clarity is desirable or even possible. Some would argue that the very nature of higher education renders its purpose indefinable, that definition itself implies limitations in the pursuit of knowledge. Yet there is not world enough and time, or money, to provide everything to all persons without boundary or limit. Nations and states pursue educational policy without a definitive understanding of what they are about and why they are providing education. Policy maker fashion elaborate schemes of objectives, methods, and evaluation without knowing what is to be taught, how to convey the education, and how to evaluate programs, but societies denote little worthwhile discussion to the question of ultimate purpose. The foundational issues of what the nation is hoping to achieve through higher education tend to float, unattached, beyond the grasp of governments, and their inability to respond becomes endemic and perpetual.

In a broader context, no less a light than Immanuel Kant observed that the duty of all people is to achieve human perfection;[3] therefore, implicitly, the role of the university should lead to that end. The duty of which Kant speaks is the obligation to cultivate one's own capacities: "Man has a duty to raise himself from a crude state of his nature, from his animality, more and more toward humanity, ... he has a duty to diminish his ignorance by instruction and to correct his errors."[4] Every person, then, has an obligation to elevate himself or herself through learning and must do so for both personal betterment and for the happines of others.[5] Thus Kant implicitly calls for education as the route to this perfectibility, "to diminish ignorance by instruction." Condorcet, at about the same time, 1793, reached a similar conclusion but placed perfectibility in the context of progress, where new knowledge increasingly elevates individuals above the state of nature.[6] Condorcet speaks of advancement of the human condition through the "freeing of the human mind from the bonds" of prejudice and ignorance.[7] He adds a twist by applying economics to the acquisition of knowledge – since Gutenberg a "brisk and universal trade" in knowledge had emerged.[8] That "universal trade" is what universities are all about – their reason for existence.

More recent discussions of the role of the university seem more pragmatic and less philosophical. In 1959, C.P. Snow postulated "The Two Cultures and the Scientific Revolution."[9] Snow, a public figure and a scientist, juxtaposed the interests of the two cultures – the sciences and the humanities. Educational institutions were not "coping with the scientific revolution" or aiding in the advancement of productive industry.[10] As Snow saw it, the interests of the humanities and social studies opposed progress in the sciences and technology, showing the advancement of science and thus inhibiting capital production and national economic development.

Snow implied that the root objective of science is to address "world-scale needs, capital: capital in all forms, including capital machinery." The "world-scale needs", as Snow saw them, were three – the H-bomb threat, overpopulation, and the gap between rich and poor. His thesis was that only advances in science and technology could allow nations to address these issues, but he was less than explicit as to how. "Our education had gone wrong"[11] by not resolving the conflict between sciences and the humanities in the universities.

Since 1959 many advances have fostered an emerging unity of knowledge, which tends to obviate Snow's assertions.[12] According to Wilson, there is an accelerating "juncture of science and the humanities,"[13] and the progress of scientific research has opened new frontiers, beyond which the natural sciences can be "united with the social sciences and humanities."[14] Such initiatives and revitalizing, the "liberal arts in higher education."[15]

However, Wilson's observations regarding Snow's thesis are delimited to the resolution of the separation of the two cultures and not with the use of science and technology to advance economic development. Wilson argues that the university's role is to foster "[a] united system of knowledge" for the purpose of "identifying the still unexplored domains of reality." The search for "consilience" is essential to the expansion of knowledge, "locating new avenues of creative thought." As for where the expansion of knowledge should lead, Wilson returns to Condorcet, noting that "the Enlightenment, despite the erosion of its original vision, and despite the shakiness of some of its premises, has been the principal inspiration not just of Western high culture, but, increasingly, of the entire world."[16] "Science was the engine of the Enlightenment,"[17] and the power of reasoning and the "torch of analysis" are the means of human perfectibility.[18]

Wilson, however, does not address the questions of right and wrong and of how we are to know the difference. After all, a scientific experiment or a mathematical formula does not cultivate appreciation of human values. In the aftermath of the Second World War, Frederic Lilge re-examined the consequences of Germany's long-standing pursuit of science and technology. In *The Abuse of Learning: The Failure of the German University*,[19] Lilge quotes the German philosopher Schelling, who argued that "a university should awaken young men's understanding of the interrelations and the unity of knowledge."[20] Wilson's "consilience" comes quite close to this objective. Yet Lilge warns against the "idolatry of science" in the university.[21] He views favourably the idea that the "progress of knowledge is the chief purpose of the university" but cautions against seeing science as *a priori* the sole means to that happy end.[22]

Lilge was sceptical about devotion to a "vaguely concealed 'cause' usually described as progress,"[23] and he worried that scientific specialization could lead to a constricted view of scientific utility incapable of distinguishing right from wrong or even of discerning what constituted human progress. Helmhotz, patron saint of science and technology, who preached that scientific discovery alone led to industrial progress and the improvement of general welfare, staunchly held that other knowledge, beyond science, could not give direction to science in the service of society. As Lilge saw it, this philosophy perpetuated a great error, and as a result German universities "mistook progress in science for universal progress."[24]

Lilge maintained in retrospect that the view of universities as merely scientific research centres produced a "human void which yawned under the bustling productivity and the moral default" and that led to the collapse of German universities and their submission to National Socialism in 1933 and after.[25] By ignoring the humanities, philosophy, and social sciences, the universities ignored the "moral life" and "value systems" of students as they invited and promoted a "heedless preoccupation"[26] with science and technology.

What this suggests is that in determining the appropriate balance between the two cultures, a state or nation cannot ignore the role and direction of the university in society, where the learning emphasis of the university lies, and its probable impact. One is irresistibly drawn to some form of Wilson's consilience that fosters science and technical progress while instilling human values and secular moral standards that temper and guide policy makers. Whatever the balance, both Lilge and Wilson would appear to agree that the university should be a bulwark against a rudderless progress that would have unforeseen and perhaps dire consequences.

States and nations therefore must define their purposes in provision for their universities. Perhaps the object of the university cannot be defined with any clarity, and in reality education may simply respond to the caprice of the particular government in power at any appointed time. A government may be vague on the subject because more specification is impossible or the superfluidity of the politics of the day ebbs and flows with such frequency that an amorphous context for higher education is not only necessary, but may even be desirable. It could possibly be quite dangerous for governmental leaders to attempt to define the university's purpose and it may be far better if such remains indefinite. Inevitably, such questions raise the spectre of control and emphasis, possibly to the detriment of free thought and expansion of knowledge. Yet, this does not necessarily obviate the need for a rational purpose and policy to achieve some desired social end.

THE PRIOR QUESTION: DOES HIGHER EDUCATION SHAPE GOVERNMENT?

A critical prior question is whether the university is destined to be merely a tool to achieve government's immediate ends or whether it is to shape government itself. Do we arrange higher education to advance governmental policy, or do we fashion educational policy to form and mould government? In Lilge's terms, is the university to be used by government to advance interests that may not have moral ends? In addressing this prior question, we find little help from Newman, Snow, even Wilson.

A realist would argue that for education to shape the government makes a presumption that denies both history and experience. The educational idealist, in contrast, would maintain that an educated people does ultimately mould its government, while an uneducated people requires less of government. The realist would maintain that government uses education to achieve its own ends and that factors other than education will determine the success or failure of both the government and education.

Thus there emerges the eternal dispute, as Albert Sorel has put it, "between those who imagine the world to suit their policy, and those who arrange their policy to suit the realities of the world."[27] Whether realism or idealism will ultimately prevail probably cannot be determined, and so any discussion of the university's ultimate purpose has inherent limitations. Yet there is an underlying credibility to the idealist position – emanating from nineteenth-century optimism – that good government will result from right reasoning, that a general increase in the diffusion of knowledge will provide the basis for people to reason rightly with regard to their own governance, and that right reason will logically lead to right actions.[28]

Both Jean-Jacques Rousseau and Kant argued that knowledgeable people supporting republican governments will realize that their best interests rest not in war but in peace. Jeremy Bentham maintained that members of the community, if given the opportunity, form the best tribunal for adjudication of social and political controversies.[29] This idealism, which Carr calls the "doctrine of salvation by public opinion,"[30] was further elaborated by James Mill, Bentham's pupil, as he circumscribed the ultimate "infallibility" of public opinion for setting governmental direction: "Every man possessed of reason is accustomed to weigh evidence and to be guided and determined by its preponderance. When various conclusions are, with the evidence, presented with equal care and with equal skill, there is a moral certainty, though some few may be misguided, that the greatest number will judge right, and that the greatest force of evidence, whatever it is, will produce the greatest impression."[31]

This argument, which is used to defend democracy, assumes that the majority cannot be misguided. Of course, objective evidence is rarely presented to the public with "equal care and equal skill," so as to prevend misdirection. Yet it is generally agreed that the better educated the people, the greater the likelihood that right reason will prevail.

What then does right reason demand of universities? Surely reason and rationality would suggest that we educate for the higher purpose of humankind. Some argue that the increase of prosperity should be a basic purpose of the university; others maintain, in contrast, that all education, primary through college, should inculcate nationalism. Each of these purposes merits consideration, and, while their logical advancement appears unassailable, closer examination below shows the issues to be less clear.

THE INCREASE OF PROSPERITY AS THE OBJECTIVE

Prosperity may come the closest of all objectives to realistic purpose. One may argue that prosperity ensures a society's stability and the retention of the status quo and that economic expansion can ease inequities. The dominant and advantaged group will always seek to maintain and preserve legitimacy in order to ensure its own prosperity. A realist view suggests that government will move towards achievement of this end.

Yet the university, in its scholastic pursuits, may not result in the obtaining of such a generally accepted end. After all, it is reasonable to assume that educated people dislike war and will eschew destructive conflict that undermines prosperity. Buckle, in his famous *History of Civilization* (1857), declared that love of peace and a dislike of war were "a cultivated taste peculiar to an intellectual people."[32]

Realism would suggest that the diffusion of knowledge does not create accord either within or among nations, but rather engenders a more elevated clamour for greater economic gain. Niebuhr has noted that self-deception and hypocrisy are less obvious in individuals than in nations.[33] In fact, the rationality that intellectual development breeds may lead to the conclusion that simple economic gain is not alone a worthy goal, but rather that there exists a higher golden mean. It is no secret that the better educated are less content to suffer deprivation than the uneducated. If the educational objective is to achieve economic superiority, then it always comes at a price.

ECONOMIC EFFICIENCY AS THE OBJECTIVE

Should the ultimate purpose of the university be economic efficiency? "The capitalist spirit is as old as history," and experience[34] suggests that nations ultimately rise or fall as a result of their economic condition.[35] An economically efficient society will be wealthier than an inefficient one.[36] Few would disagree with Tawney, who said, "The virtues of enterprise, diligence, and thrift are the indispensable foundation of any complex and vigorous society."[37] The demise of communism and the fall of the Soviet Union are striking historical examples of a failed economic policy.

Failure of economic growth has always been a factor in the rise and fall of nations, and the decline of many great powers has been testimony to economic as much as to military failure. Commerce had been Britain's strength, and it would prove to be its critical weakness. Power does have much to do with the choice of economic policy. The maintenance and extension of overseas markets and the ability to broaden fields of investment have spelled the success or failure of developing and developed countries.[38]

Apostles of free trade have attached to it a certain morality, and some have even characterized capitalism in terms of a moral calling, attributing an extraordinary, almost religious, character to the economic efficiency of free trade. Cobden, in 1870, saw benefits to capitalism that reached beyond wealth and prosperity to engender a kind of moral code. He said that free trade acted "on the moral world as the principle of gravitation in the universe – drawing men together, thrusting aside the antagonism of race, and creed, and language, and uniting us in the bonds of external peace."[39] Such testimonials in the Western world are too numerous to cite.

The point here is simply that economic interests are an indisputable wellspring of international power and respect, and it is around this purpose that a nation's university pursuits will tend to collect and germinate.

The present-day advancement of the North American Free Trade Agreement (NAFTA) and the World Trade Organization (WTO) is a strong testimonial to the power of *laissez-faire* economics. To a lesser extent, some Far East and European states follow this rule with some degree of leavening sanctioned by adherents of Frederick List who argue for governmental intervention and protection in certain circumstances. Even assuming a measure of governmental activity to regulate markets, many see competitive capitalism as the route to advancing the economic condition and the state of civilization. Much of the world has apparently adopted the philosophy expressed so clearly by John Stuart Mill when he said, "*Laisser-faire* ... should be the general practice; every departure from it, unless required by some great good, is a certain evil."[40] These considerations have gained such credence in recent years that the World Bank, the OECD, the European Union, and individual nations make much of the connection between the growth of knowledge and economic productivity. The *Economist* has stated that good economic policy promotes good governmental policy and that there are indisputable links between better education and economic growth: "[A] competitive microeconomy furthers educational progress because it raises the economic returns from extra years of schooling; equally, better education makes the economy more competitive by making workers more productive."[41] The strong link between the level of educational achievement and growth in productivity is well established; "Countries with a high level of education tend to absorb new technology more quickly and so grow more rapidly."[42]

Without question, education is related to economic growth, and the better educated the people, the higher its standard of living. To acknowledge this fact, however, does not necessarily mean that higher education should inculcate *laissez-faire* capitalism and that the university should seek to instill in each scholar the dogma of competition.

Universities, many would argue, should have a purpose that transcends mere economic efficiency. *Laissez-faire* economics may conceivably threaten the expansion of liberty, equality, and commonality. A state or a nation perhaps cannot reject the competitive economic model without devaluing "enterprise, diligence and thrift" as desirable human characteristics. It is one thing to teach that "thrift" and the careful use of resources are preferable to profligacy, yet quite another to inculcate the *laissez-faire* competitive model as a ground for human motivations. Pareto optimality and supply and demand curves have the same inability as scientific formulas and mathematical models to determine what is good or bad, moral or immoral, ethical or unethical. To allow economic determination to be a holy grail risks the fostering of a society with a limited value perspective – a society without a sustaining eleemosynary spirit and possibly devoid of the values of sacrifice and charity. In such circumstances the basic and inherent need for social equality may go unheeded and unappreciated.

The marketplace itself tends to generate inequality. According to Kuttner, "By market standards, inequality is not a regrettable necessity, but a virtue."[43] To inculcate the ideals of capitalism may be only a short step from governmental reinforcement of humanity's primitive and uncivilized tendencies towards self-interest, greed, and avarice. If it is true, as H.L.A. Hart says, that in nature "human altruism is limited in range and intermittent"[44] or, as Samuel Alexander once said, that "man's humanity to man is a very thin veneer," then achievement of a higher social order surely requires some effective harnessing of humanity and society's "selfish" gene.[45]

The dilemma for the planners of university policy is to determine to what extent they should design the intellectual force of the university to reinforce humankind's competitive urges, which may be simultaneously constructive and destructive. To what extent should universities instill the importance of self-interest as a way of advancing both the individual and society's economic condition?

It would seem then that the purpose of the university should not be to fuel humanity's natural "asocial" tendencies to competition and self-interest, but rather to teach the salutary effects of economic efficiency within the context of the more basic human interests of liberty, equality, and commonality of social interests. The purpose of universities may well be to restrain extremes of self-interest and to encourage common accord, economic stability, and harmony in the social condition. It would seem further that their purpose should not be to exacerbate discord, but rather to mitigate self-interest and to teach the "necessity of mutual forbearance and compromise which is the base of both legal and moral obligation."[46] Higher education should certainly not dampen the competitive urge, but rather channell and order the capitalist spirit to raise the standard of living while reducing the more deleterious aspects of competition.

THE UNIVERSITY AS A TOOL OF GOVERNMENT

One of the most commonly enunciated purposes of education is the creating of strength in states and nations. Sir Christopher Ball has observed that a frequently given reason for maintaining an educational system is for socialization, which has been widely interpreted in both East and West as an aspect of advancement of nationalism. He notes that "some eastern countries redefine socialization as 'national unity' and consider its achievement as the first function of education."[47] He further observes that in the West, too, nationalism and the promotion of a common culture are often identified as a purpose of universities.[48]

Regardless of region, much governmental action reflects the nationalistic purpose of education. For example, it is no secret that a principal objective of the Soviet Union's education system was to reduce cultural differences in the Soviet republics and to consolidate Russian hegemony. As a result, after the fall of the Soviet Union, Belarus, the Ukraine, Georgia, and the other republics set in motion educational reforms that would reverse past Soviet influence and restore their own identities. V.A. Gaisyonok has written:

Within the past four decades the national school (of Belarus) has been completely destroyed. Despite the fact the Byelorussians account for 80 percent of the republic's population, the instruction in 80 percent of all schools was in Russian ... In the 1930s, a considerable part of the nation's intelligentsia was accused of nationalism by the Stalin regime and wiped out. Following that, science developed in Belarus primarily as an item of Russian export and culture would be identified as the culture of the Russian people.[49]

The conflict over nationalism is not confined to the former Soviet republics. In his Pulitzer Prize-winning study of American education, Cremin classifies the era from 1783 to 1876 as "The National Experience."[50] "Governments have a considerable domestic interest in mobilizing nationalism among its citizens,"[51] and education has served as an essential tool to forge national pride. States have used the powerful machinery of mass education "to spread the image and heritage of the 'nation' and to attach the citizenry to it. In order to do this traditions are invented, attaching the country and flag, patriotic songs are written and sung, flags are flown and stirring poems and stories are passed on about heros and their deeds."[52]

We see daily evidences of a nation's seeking to enhance a nationalistic spirit by means of various devices. Today, France is experiencing internal political turmoil over the purity of its nationalism as affected by religion, language, and multiculturalism. The French government has even deported Turkish Muslims who supported Moroccan ideals and religious beliefs.[53] Such acts, officials conjectured, would presumably spread unchecked and create divisive influences in the nationalist spirit of France. A government spokesman sought to justify such actions: "Now, for the first time, we have people born in France who are not French."[54] Prime Minister Edouard Balladur acted to limit immigration in order to reduce the perceived "threat" of immigrants' further eroding the "purity" of the French culture.

Similar concerns have arisen in the United States, where some commentators have maintained that multicultural and multi-ethnic influences will undermine the nation's internal structure. Kaplan observes: "[I]t is not clear that the United States will survive the next century in its present form. Because America is a multiethnic society, it has always been more fragile than more homogeneous societies like Germany and Japan."[55]

After the Second World War, many East Germans dreamed of nationalism in the face of Soviet domination. The Federal Republic of Germany[56] saw nationalism as desirable, but untenable, so long as reunification was out of reach.[57] In East Germany, as throughout eastern Europe, there transpired "the very strange phenomenon of a mass shift in the loyalty of intellectuals from communism to nationalism."[58] Then, with the surprising reality of reunification, the German people moved to bear the economic and social consequences of a re-established national unity. Today, through re-education and economic sacrifice, a new era of nationalism is emerging.

The thrust of neonationalism is probably as potent in the world today as it has ever been. The disaster in the Balkans and the continuous strife in parts of Africa, India, and the Middle East offer striking evidence of the stridency of ill-conceived nationalism.

Well aware of the barbarism attributable to virulent nationalism, Dunn has observed: "Nationalism is the starkest political shame of the twentieth century, the deepest, most intractable and, yet, most unanticipated blot on the political history of the world since the 1900s."[59] The ethical accord envisaged in Rousseau's theoretical construct has, in Dunn's view, become a vehicle of blatant immorality in the light of practical realism.

From the mid-nineteenth century onward, nations have been formed and reformed in terms of geographical boundaries, ethnic lines, cultural history, language, and religious beliefs – some agreeable vision of community. All those nations, large or small, have some ideological foundation that sustains them. Dunn wrote: "There is no state today so ramshackled that it cannot muster an ideological proclamation of why its citizens should trust it"[60] (and cast their lives and fortunes to support it) and inculcate this suspect value by means of its education system.

Political leaders realize that they must influence and fashion individual wills in such a way as to strengthen the general will and that the university is probably the highest and best resource for effectuating this end.

As Niebuhr observed, "The selfishness of nations is proverbial."[61] "Nations cannot be trusted beyond their own interest," argued George Washington.[62] History suggests an inherent contradiction between nationalism and virtue.

In this light, then, the purpose of the university cannot be simply to advance the desire of government to feed a nationalistic spirit without heed to what that spirit entails. Rather, the ideal is for the university, through a "unity of knowledge," to engender a desirable liberal nationalism. For the university to teach undefined or indifferent nationalism in a society of collective immorality and intolerance, as we have seen in the Balkans and Vietnam, is untenable from any rational perspective. The university then should not be the blind tool of government, but should have more basic and profound moral and ethical foundations.

CONCLUSION

As the discussion above indicates, there are few obvious answers to the question, "What is the object of the university?" Even though strengthing the nation would be relatively unimpeachable, closer examination reveals serious problems.

The desirability of thrift and efficiency in both the individual and government cannot be doubted, and those principles are most

worthwhile and essential, but education should distinguish constructive efficiency from avarice bred by predatory self-interest. If we are
to believe Hobbes, Hegel, Locke, and Adam Smith – and many in the
North Atlantic would give substantial weight to such opinions – we
must conclude that individuals are primarily self-interested, self-
actualizing, and egotistical in their social and economic pursuits. To
understand this as preordained by Smith's "invisible hand" but
blindly reinforce its undesirable propensities through higher education is the antithesis of intellectual development. The university must
strive to reach beyond being merely a collective of separate, unintel-
lectual pursuits of self-interests. As Angell, president of the University
of Michigan, once said: "The obstacle in our path ... is not in the
moral sphere, but in the intellectual ... It is not because men are
illdisposed that they cannot be educated into a world social con-
sciousness. It is because they ... are beings of conservative temper
and limited intelligence."[63]

In Angell's view, humanity's natural tendency towards pride,
ambition, and greed is exacerbated by "muddled thinking."[64] A positive intellectual development should mitigate these more primitive
instincts, not strengthen them. For the university to reinforce them is
to further undesirable propensities. What good does it do society to
provide higher education if only to foster an innate and strong-willed
aggressive egotism?

Similarly, the motive of the university cannot be to advance nationalism without examining its underlying motivations and concepts in
the light of more basic considerations such as virtue, morality, liberty, and equality. On balance, nationalism may be considered a negative social force, even though a realist would conclude that it is
inevitable. Second World War experiences and today's sorry state of
affairs in the Balkans and Northern Ireland are merely selected
examples. The solution cannot be to pursue an educational policy of
"narrow nationalism"; rather, higher education must be designed to
ameliorate intolerance and to advance rationality and forbearance.[65]

What then should be the broad "object of the university"? First and
foremost, it should be understood that education is a fundamental
right and that development of knowledge is the prerequisite to a
desirable state of civilization. Enlightenment and expansion of
knowledge should be the rule, and higher education should oppose
"contracting the spectrum of knowledge." The narrow channeling
of thought and the central control of educational objectives create

conditions that restrict expansiveness of learning, and therefore production of rational thought and the scientific method should be vigorously protected.

University education should be seen as the primary advanced means to develop the intellect, expand the horizons of knowledge, and prepare youths for a life of contribution and sacrifice in building a democratic society based on virtue. University education should have as a major objectives the breaking down of barriers of class and the moderating of intergenerational privilege and personal aggrandizement. The allure of the university to the individual should not be enhancement of economic and social status and exploitation of the less advantaged; instead it should inculcate the value of merit in personal achievements and obligation. "The [university] should be permeated, not with the competitive, but with the cooperative, spirit. It should strive to serve society as a whole, to promote the most inclusive interests."[66] At the same time, higher education must promote the full development of individual talents and provide the climate and incentives for personal betterment through pursuit of knowledge. In this light, the public university system should be designed to accommodate individuals' varying educational needs and to advance a collective aspiration for expansion of knowledge.

Moreover, the motivation of a university education should not be to espouse moral platitudes that bear little relationship to the condition of civil reality. Disengaged enunciations of "virtues" that are daily contradicted by deed and practice are not only futile, but hypocritical and dishonest. A former U.S. secretary of education, William Bennett, has published a number of edited books[67] on "virtues," while at the same time encouraging disregard for civil rights laws, reduction of funding for public schools, and economic and social segregation through funding of privileged children attending private schools.

Possibly, the most important purpose of education should be to inculcate tolerance for differences in race, religion, culture, language, nationality, and ethnic origin. The university should define and teach the difference between peace for oppression and peace for liberty, the difference between competitive, self-interested capitalism and a *laissez-faire* spirit that provides for a "harmony, broad based and "liberal"[68] nationalism. The brand of patriotism that is founded on intolerance – a "narrow" or "illiberal" nationalism – should be singled out by the educational process as being undesirable and in the best interest of neither the individual nor the nation. Historical proofs should be constantly advanced that inveigh against bigotry, genetic preference, and religious intolerance in the name of nationalism.

The public university system should advance the ideal of interdependence and commonality both within and among nations and states, and education should arm humankind in its struggle against the natural primitive instincts of the Hobbesian state of nature and to glorify and honour the common interest and the common weal.

NOTES

This chapter is adapted from an unpublished paper concerning the purpose of education given at the Oxford Round Table.

1 John Henry Newman, *The Idea of a University Defined and Illustrated*, I, in *Nine Discourses Delivered to the Catholics of Dublin* (1852); II. In *Occasional Lectures and Essays Addressed to the members of the Catholic University* (1858), ed. with introduction and notes by I.T. Ker (Oxford: Clarendon Press, 1976).

2 Jaroslav Pelikan, *The Idea of the University: A Reexamination* (New Haven, Conn.: Yale University Press, 1992). In his preface, Newman defines the university as "a place of teaching" and as a community of scholars – a "mansion-house of the goodly family of the Sciences, sisters all, and sisterly in their mutual dispositions."

3 Immanuel Kant, *The Metaphysics of Morals*, first pub. 1797 (Cambridge: Cambridge University Press, 1993), 191.

4 Ibid., 191. Kant maintains that "morally practical reason commands it absolutely and makes this his duty, so that he may be worthy of the humanity that dwells within him."

5 Ibid., 192.

6 Edward Goodell, *The Noble Philosopher: Condorcet and the Enlightenment* (Buffalo, NY: Prometheus Books, 1994), 215.

7 Ibid.

8 See *Sketch for a Historical Picture of the Progress of the Human Mind*, trans. June Barraclough (New York: Noonday Press, 1955; reprint: Westport, Conn.: Hyperion Press, 1978), 99.

9 C.P. Snow, *The Two Cultures* (Cambridge: Cambridge University Press, 1959).

10 Ibid., 33.

11   Ibid., 34.
12   Edward O. Wilson, *Consilience: The Unity of Knowledge* (New York: Vintage Books, 1998).
13   Ibid., 243.
14   Ibid., 294.
15   Ibid.
16   Ibid., 24.
17   Ibid.
18   Ibid.
19   Frederic Lilge, *The Abuse of Learning: The Failure of the German University,* first pub. 1948 (New York: Octagon Books, 1975).
20   Ibid., 42.
21   Ibid., 57–83.
22   Ibid., 71.
23   Ibid., 74.
24   Ibid., 76.
25   Ibid., 77.
26   Ibid., 76.
27   Albert Sorel, *L'Europe et la Revolution Française,* (Paris: 1904), 474.
28   Edward Hallett Carr, *The Twenty Years Crisis, 1919–1939* (New York: Harper & Row, 1939), 24–5.
29   Jeremy Bentham, *Works, the Public Opinion Tribuna,* ed. Bowring, viii, 561.
30   Carr, *Crisis,* 24.
31   James Mill, *The Liberty of the Press,* 22–3.
32   Cited by Norman Angell, *Foundations of International Polity* (London: Heinemann, 1914), 224.
33   Reinhold Niebuhr, *Moral Man and Immoral Society* (New York: Charles Scribner's Sons, 1932), 95.
34   R.H. Tawney, *Religion and the Rise of Capitalism,* first pub. 1926 (London: Penquin Books, 1990), 225.
35   "Capitalism" may be defined as the tendency towards and acceptance of an economic system in which all or most of the means of production and distribution are privately owned and operated for profit, and it generally leads to concentration of wealth and inequality of incomes.
36   Richard A. Posner, *The Economics of Justice* (Cambridge, Mass.: Harvard University Press, 1981), 205.
37   Tawney, *Religion.*
38   Bernard Porter, *The Lion's Share: A Short History of British Imperialism, 1850–1983* (London: Longman, 1984), 142.

39 Richard Cobden, *Speeches on Questions of Public Policy* (1870), ii, 135, in ibid., 6.

40 John Stuart Mill, *Principles of Political Economy*, vol. II (Boston: Charles Little & James Brown, 1848), book V, chap. xi, p. 524.

41 "The Path to Growth," *Economist*, 13–19 July 1991, 77.

42 "Economic Focus," ibid., 12–18 Sept. 1992, 75.

43 Robert Kuttner, *The Economic Illusion: False Choices between Prosperity and Social Justice* (Philadelphia: University of Pennsylvania Press, 1991), 10.

44 H.L.A. Hart, *The Concept of Law* (Oxford: Clarendon Press, 1961), 191–2.

45 See T.H. Marshall, as quoted in Kuttner, *Illusion*, 15.

46 Hart, *Concept*, 191.

47 Sir Christopher Ball, "Making Sense of the Reform and Restructuring of Education and Training," in *The Faces of Education: A World View* (Murray, Ky.: Oxford Round Table on Education Policy, 1995), 7–16.

48 Ibid.

49 V.A. Gaisyonok, Minister of Education, Oxford Round Table.

50 Lawrence A. Cremin, *American Education: The National Experience, 1783–1876* (New York: Harper & Row, 1980).

51 E.J. Hobsbawm, *Nations and Nationalism since 1780* (Cambridge: Cambridge University Press, 1990), 91.

52 E.J. Hobsbawm, "Mass-producing Tradition: Europe 1870–1914," in E.J. Hobsbawm and T. Ranger, eds., *The Invention of Tradition* (Cambridge: Cambridge University Press, 1983), chap. 7.

53 Alan Riding, "France, Reversing Course, Fights Immigrants' Refusal to Be French," *New York Times*, 5 Dec. 1993.

54 Commentary by Jean-Claude Barreau, a representative of the French government, in ibid.

55 Robert D. Kaplan, "The Coming Anarchy," *Atlantic Monthly*, Feb. 1994, 76.

56 Anne-Marie Le Glaoanneec, "On German Identity," *Daedalus* 123, no. 1 (winter 1994), 136.

57 Ibid.

58 John Kifner, *New York Times*, Sunday 10 April 1994.

59 John Dunn, *Western Political Theory in the Face of the Future*, Canto edition (Cambridge: University of Cambridge Press, 1993), 57.

60 Ibid., 64.

61 Niebuhr, *Moral Man*, 84.

62 Ibid.

63 Sir Norman Angell, *Neutrality and Collective Security*, Harris Foundation Lectures (Chicago: University of Chicago Press, 1936), 8, 18.

64 Ibid.

65 Elie Kedourie, *Nationalism* (Oxford: Blackwells Publishers, 1993), 62.
66 George S. Counts, *The Social Foundations of Education* (New York: Charles Scribner's Sons, 1934), 542.
67 William J. Bennett, *The Book of Virtues: A Treasury of Moral Stories* (New York: Simon & Schuster, 1993).
68 Michael Lind, "In Defense of Liberal Nationalism," *Foreign Affairs* 73, no. 3 (May–June 1994), 94.

Reinventing Universities in Australia

DON AITKIN

My text is a simple one: it is true that the university is one of society's oldest institutions, and the principal reason for its longevity, I maintain, is that it has learned to adapt to contemporary needs. I go further to argue that the last 150 years has seen periods of adaptation and that we are undergoing one now. All such accommodations are resisted by most of those who inhabit the institution, as one would expect. I argue for some understanding of this process and some realization that without change the university would be bypassed by other competitor institutions in some or all of its functions, which university people would regret.

The kinds of change of which I am writing usually lack defined starting and ending moments, especially in the last fifty years. But we ourselves are likely to supply such markers – major government reports and acts of parliaments are traditional ones. As I explain below, I think that the process is much more subtle and continuous than such markers suggest. The demands placed on universities by society grow and change without much reference to government decisions, which seem always to come afterwards, as a kind of official recognition that something needed to be done.

Let me start with some history. Only a few years ago the academic world celebrated the 900th anniversary of the University of Bologna – the oldest continuously operating institution of higher education in the world. But in the 1090s that institution was not much like my own university or that of most people here, having evolved out of a cathedral school, possessing no buildings or permanent site, and offering no degrees. The earliest universities were able to chart a course independently of the church through charters issued by popes or kings. For all that, one of their principal purposes was training young men for a career, either in the church or in the state. That is still the principal function of universities, except that we now train young women too, and we help graduates to advance in their profession or to shift from one profession to another.

It is architecture that plays the greatest part in inducing us to see universities as unchanging. Oxford University appears as an ancient seat of learning because many of its buildings are very old, and it is tempting to assume that life within the cloisters has always been the same. But of course it has not been. Balliol, which now has perhaps the most intellectually ambitious students in Oxford, was founded as a place for "artists," and the oldest colleges were little more than endowed boarding-houses. And while "science" was professed there as early as the thirteenth century in the person of Roger Bacon, students in European universities – in most cases, up into the eighteenth century – studied grammar, logic, and rhetoric before moving on to law, medicine, or theology.

Changes to curriculum arising from the Enlightenment were slow in coming. The "modern" university owes a great deal more to Karl Wilhelm von Humboldt in early nineteenth-century Prussia and his American admirers than it does to earlier traditions. The early-modern university survived because society needed its products and because most universities "kept their heads down." Not all of them survived, but those that had useful land generally did or merged with other, similar institutions.

What we take to be the "traditional" university in Britain, Canada, the United States, and Australia is very much a creation of the nineteenth century, especially the latter part. The serious study by undergraduates of the natural sciences in a laboratory is even more recent – largely an early-twentieth-century innovation. So too is the study of English literature and of modern languages – in fact, of the humanities generally, always excepting philosophy and classics. The great social sciences may be a little older, since their principal journals date started in the 1880s.

Just as universities in early modern times had to establish their independence both from the church and from the state yet maintain good relations with both, so that their independence was not under continual threat, so have modern universities needed to adapt to the changes that have overtaken humanity in the last two centuries. The great growth of population, urbanization, the industrial revolution, the movement towards democracy, successive improvements in useful technologies, a greater scientific understanding of the basis of reality – changes that characterize the nineteenth century, although all remain important – led to the development of the social sciences and the sciences. Universities were not to the fore in these developments, so far as I can see: they were slow to respond. In fact, the universities needed to be reformed before they could become part of the modern world – this is certainly what happened in Oxford.

TWENTIETH-CENTURY CHANGES

There were four major changes in the twentieth century to which universities in Australia, like those in other Western countries, had to adapt; all occurred after 1950. I use Australian examples, but I think that you will all recognize the trends.

The first trend was a shift in purpose, and once again the war was a primary stimulus: universities became involved in research – an activity not previously the province of Australia's universities, although it was the *raison d'être* of the Commonwealth Scientific and Industrial Research Organisation (CSIRO), set up in 1926. Research had aided the country's successful war effort, and the Australian National University (ANU) was founded in 1946 to ensure a domestic high-quality research institute. But it was not until the late 1950s, with establishment of the Commonwealth Postgraduate Scholarships and of funding for research infrastructure in the universities, followed in 1964 by creation of the Australian Research Grants Committee (ARGC), that research could be thought an ordinary occupation of all academics.

The second was a shift in scale: after the Second World War, for a variety of reasons, governments expanded universities to provide more places, and the community itself began to see further education as a proper pathway for its children, rather than favouring an early exit from education to paid work. "Children" now included girls as well as boys.

The third tendency was a further shift in scale, as the various professions, traditional and emerging, realized that only moving professional training from the workplace to higher education would ensure an appropriate share of talented young people. This change was acceptable to governments, which were the principal (after 1974, the only) financial supporters of higher education. Preparing professionals has always been a central role for universities, especially in Australia, where a professional class had to be created to ease reliance on immigration. That, not cherishing the flame of pure intellect under the Southern Cross, is the best explanation for Australia's nineteenth-century foundations.

The fourth shift involved a set of changes in funding arrangements, and I leave that until last. There is a fifth, which I leave for discussion elsewhere – "globalization."

The two changes in scale (expansion and professional training) and one of purpose (research) have had a powerful effect on the world-view of Australia's academics. The country now has some 32,000 academics, and they constitute a large profession that is national in its range, articulate (of course!), and critical, rather than supportive, of the existing order. They see themselves – correctly, in my view – as having been indispensable or instrumental in the shaping of the nation in the last half-century. In particular, they see research as something on which they have a unique handle, especially in "pure" research, which they see as the basis of all understanding, and therefore as the basis of modern life. They are also likely to see themselves – and this has probably been the chief sin of scholars and clerics since the beginning of these occupations – as more than a tad smarter and wiser than ordinary people.

Above all, they believe that they know better than anyone else how universities work, that universities are different from all other institutions, that universities, like bedrooms, are not places into which the state should seek to enter, and that universities should be left alone – except for being "properly funded" (which always involves more money than is currently available) – to do their work, which is in everybody's interest. They often couch these beliefs in the language of tradition and point to an immemorial past or at least to the universities of Bologna or Oxford or Paris. All academics of any consequence know a good deal about the intellectual history of their own field of work, and that adds a further sense of continuity. Such an intellectual history becomes pretty general for most fields if it goes back much before 1950, let alone before 1900.

The university world today is very different from that of 1950, let alone that of 1100. Over the last half-century Australia's universities have moved from being peripheral to national life to being central. Student numbers have increased from 30,000 to nearly 700,000. Budget outlays in 1950 were small; today they exceed $5 billion. In 1950 Australia was for the most part outside the world of research; it is now a notable research performer. The quantity of human knowledge available in books and journals is some fifty times greater than was the case in 1950. The quality of graduates seems high in world terms, and universities attract scores of thousands of students from more than seventy countries. Australia's sense of itself – its standing as a curious, tolerant, progressive, open democracy – has been shaped by the work of its universities and their graduates. Fifty years ago, most university students were male, young, and full-time; now most are female, many study part time, and students receive their education in a great variety of forms. To go to university is now the common expectation of the great majority of eighteen year olds.

RESEARCH

Because the buildings look the same, and campuses age more or less gracefully, it does not always occur to people that Australia's universities have been reinventing themselves and their purposes throughout this period. I can speak about this process with some confidence, because I am approaching my fiftieth year in higher education. That I am an academic at all flows from the decision of the Robert Menzies's government, following the advice of the Murray Committee in 1958, to set up a Commonwealth Postgraduate Scholarship scheme. I won one of the first scholarships, and without it I would have followed family tradition and become a high school teacher. My lecturers in 1954 were all interested in research, and eventually published, but the research environment in which they worked was tiny by today's standards. There was, for example, no Australian publishing industry of any consequence; there were few journals, and few of Australia's major academic journals had been started. People interested in research that did not have an Australian focus were separated by a six-week boat journey from the world's centres of research – it was not until the mid-1960s, and the arrival of the Boeing 707, that air travel became the accepted way to move around the world and brought Australia into the European and North American research cultures.

The universities preoccupation with research, postgraduate education, research funding and research grants, pro vice-chancellors (research), industrial partnerships, international research links, and the PhD industry and the anxieties that flow from it is all a form of invention. Over a period of a generation, the Australian university transformed itself into a knowledge-generating as well as a knowledge-transmitting institution. It became international in its perspective and contributed enormously to Australians' sense of who they were and what they had achieved.

One can put markers on this process – the foundation of the ANU in 1946, the Murray Committee of 1958, establishment of the ARGC in 1964 – but these dates reveal a slow and continuous process. Indeed, while the formal dedication in the late 1980s and early 1990s of the newer universities to research shows the continuity of the invention, research in these universities started much earlier.

EXPANSION

The ways in which universities organize research tell us something about their date of origin. The process of establishing a university anywhere (but I concentrate on Australia) is complex. Older institutions usually provide models, so the oldest Australian creations usually chose Scottish models. But there are also things to be done, or processes to employ, that fit local needs and circumstances and are grafted on. Perhaps, too, the older model has weaknesses or faults that the founders wish to avoid.

So Macquarie University, set up in the late 1960s, stressed teaching and students, because its founders thought that Sydney University undervalued them. Macquarie, like Griffith University (also a creation of the 1960s), began with multi-disciplinary schools, and not with departments, so as to avoid departmental monopolies in the shaping or reshaping of degree programs. Macquarie and Canberra (which borrowed the idea from Macquarie) adopted American units, credit-points, and semesters for organizing teaching, rather than the existing, British-inspired courses and terms, to suit degree programs that were expanding quickly to accommodate new knowledge and new demands.

The new creations received progressively less funding, as the Commonwealth government kept changing its views on what constituted a university. Only Monash and New South Wales (formed out of an older university, itself a re-invented technical college) benefited from the first flush of financial enthusiasm that followed the Murray Report in the late 1950s. The next generation, in the mid- to late 1960s, received rather less money, and the creations of the 1970s, less money still. The consequences – in library resources, scale of buildings, comprehensiveness of programs, and so on – are still apparent. What was involved here were changing views on the part of the Commonwealth government and its advisers about what constituted a type-I university. The last set of creations, those of the late 1980s and early 1990s – reinvented colleges of advanced education – received very little additional money at all. By and large, they were expected to become fully-fledged universities under their own steam, in part because they were thought to have been "universities" for some time already.

The government's own view of universities had changed even further with its dismissal both of the binary system and of the underlying assumption that there were different types of students and (therefore) of higher education.

Each set of newer creations had much in common with earlier institutions but showed some marked differences too. In time, the differences became blurred because of extensive imitation. Together the universities constitute an Australian subspecies of the world species of universities.

My own judgment, based on a good deal of experience of universities in my own country and elsewhere, is that, setting aside the ANU's Institute of Advanced Studies, which is *sui generis*, the members of the Australian group are all more alike than any one of them is like a member of another national subspecies. Notwithstanding claims of some to special excellence, Australian universities have a very great deal in common, and what is common is much more important than what is different.

PROFESSIONAL TRAINING

The changes in scale and purpose were associated with another broad change – the movement of professional training from the workplace to higher education. Once again, this is not a process with an obvious starting point, let alone any kind of finish. Law, medicine, and theology have been associated with universities from the very beginning, and in the nineteenth century engineering and architecture joined them, followed by agriculture and education. In the twentieth century professions formed out of new disciplines, such as economics, psychology, and public administration. By mid-century it was common to conceive of the university as – to use an American metaphor – a college of arts and sciences surrounded by a set of professional schools, and the University of Sydney and the University of Melbourne both fitted that model. But the extraordinary growth in "knowledge" (that is, what academics discover) of the last fifty years has spun off a large new set of disciplines and professions, all tracing origins back to the old college of arts and sciences, but busily developing their own independent existences, research paradigms, postgraduate programs, international conferences, named chairs, and so on. The list would astonish an academic of the 1950s: accounting, chiropractic, computing, defence studies, ecology, human resource development, information management, landscape, management, marketing, nursing, occupational therapy, optometry, police studies, prison studies, public relations, tourism … The list is not endless, but it shows no sign of stopping.

It is easy to be scornful of the newest arrivals, as it was in older days, when English literature was added to degree programs or faculties of education appeared. When I went off to be a professor at Macquarie in 1971, my subject, political science, was the newest kid on that block and the object of occasional loftiness from those already established. This situation ended with the later arrival of sociology, which, it was widely agreed, had no place in a real university – it was not about anything at all, a kid could do it, kids were doing it, and so on. I have encountered many versions of these attitudes over time – physicists who think that the only interesting bits of chemistry are the physics bits (the rest is only for technicians), chemists who say something comparable about geology, people in the humanities who raise their eyebrows about tourism or management without recognizing that these are both areas of applied humanities and social science. What these attitudes demonstrate, above all, is the pervading uncertainty of academics about their own work and its ultimate worth, which is the rock on which peer review rests.

Loftiness about other places and other disciplines, usually in the absence of much knowledge of either, is one of our besetting sins as a profession. It flows from uncertainty – about oneself, one's discipline, one's university – and also from the long time spent investing in one's human capital, which makes other disciplines and other universities appear as competitors rather than as colleagues.

This almost generic suspicion and distrust can make collegial life difficult, make it awkward for us to act together politically or to market together internationally, and give us a bad reputation with members of the general public, who cannot imagine why we sometimes behave as we do. Those my age can remember the scorn of those at Sydney and Melbourne for the people setting up new institutions at Kensington ("the Tech," or "the shop") and Clayton ("the farm"). Ten years or so later, there was united disdain for Macquarie ("just a teachers college") and La Trobe ("more professors than students"). I need say little about the attitudes of the older nineteen institutions to "Dawkins universities," named after the minister who finally recognized that the binary system of higher education made no sense. Yet many of these newer universities are doing very well, and their standards are no less high.

In ten years' time no doubt we will fuss about the pushiness of today's technical colleges as they too become universities. We never seem to learn – an odd criticism of universities – but then they are not conspicuous examples of "learning institutions." As Vice-Chancellor A.P. Rowe of the University of Adelaide pointed out forty years ago, we "show great reluctance to undertake any research into [our] own affairs or to face changes in a spirit of experiment" (*If the Gown Fits*, Melbourne 1960, 14).

FUNDING

I come now to the last of the big changes – to funding. This one too has occurred in Europe and North America, and we can supply markers – most notably, the Australian budget of 1996, which began an explicit "down-sizing" of the universities. In the previous year the Labor government decided not to fund salary increases in higher education and to let the universities and the unions slug it out in "enterprise bargaining," which neither occurs in the enterprise nor is really a bargain. Even earlier, in 1987, the Labor government ended funding for overseas students at Australian universities and indicated that universities could charge them fees if they wished. Of course, they wished. An earlier government's budgets of the early

1980s slowly but steadily reduced funding for students in higher education – a process that continues today.

There is not, of course, any "correct" way to fund universities. Practices differ from country to country, and in the same country over time. Australia has known a fee-based system, mixed fees and government support, a wholly government sole support, and several other combinations of fees and government support. Whether citizens prefer public or private funding depends on a mix of ideological and personal factors. As university participation increases, it can be seen as a further stage in education and therefore as a proper recipient of public funds, or the argument for a substantial private contribution may grow stronger as more people participate: why should those who do not attend pay taxes to support those who do, when university graduates are likely to earn higher incomes anyway?

There seems little doubt to me that the present government and its predecessor correctly judged that they could change funding without losing votes. The university system has been unable and unprepared to argue its case in a united and cogent way, for reasons that I outlined above. I therefore expect our present funding regime to continue for some time. It has led to a further reinvention of universities, this time as private rather than as public institutions, or, if you like, as another kind of "mixed" institution, like the Australian telecommunications company, Telstra, or the public–private Commonwealth Bank. On the whole, this is not a change whose direction I support, but as a vice-chancellor I have no real option: if my university has to be a business, then it had better be a successful business.

And this kind of reinvention must lead to a lot of rethinking about what we are for and what we do. A fee-based university – for that is what is surely in prospect – has to think about what students want and provide it – always, of course, from the perspective of the disinterested professional (for we are a profession). Collectively, we need to recognize that the more successful we are in enrolling and graduating students, the more we change our society. To some extent, the postmodern, consumer-based society is itself a creation of the universities. The professional neoclassical economists who drive government policies are all products of universities, and the philosophical basis of these policies has both been taught within universities and reinforced within a global economy whose operation is based substantially on neoclassical principles. As universities reinvent themselves, they will also reinvent the society that their graduates will transform. Universities are too powerful to live outside society any longer.

CONCLUSION

We ought, I think, to see reinvention as a natural process, argue for the right way or ways to accomplish it, and take charge of the process. We need to capture the imagination and interest of our community in a new way, not as monopolists of knowledge and credentials, for we are losing that position quickly, but as institutions whose eyes are on the future and on the knowledge and education that will be necessary. We need to see our alumni as our allies and partners, not as merely sources of donations or defenders of the status quo. We need to discover what it costs to do what we do, to charge properly for it, and if necessary to find better ways of doing it. We need to align ourselves with the future, not with the past.

Many academics hate the whole process, and resist it, hoping that in the long run government will come to its senses or that something good will happen to change the context in which all this occurs. From time to time I share these sentiments, for I am a product of the last great nation-building episode in our history and find it hard to accept a perspective that suggests that nation-building is over and that we need now to concentrate on our private lives. But I know that my university will adapt, because it has already done so successfully. All our universities will do so, faster or slower, according to case, to past history, and to available incentives.

What is essential is for the present generation of university staff to capture the spirit of their university, its sense of its own purpose, and character, and virtue, and reinvent all that for the future. If we can do that, we can provide to those who come after us, and to our society, a strong, resilient, and useful university system that the society values and supports, in whatever mixture of public and private funding happens to rule at the time.

Yes, reinvention is a hard thing to do. But it has to be done. As I have shown, the last fifty years has seen almost-continuous reinvention. It has produced a modern, excellent, accessible, and attractive set of universities, which we now must further reshape for the twenty-first century. I am sure that we will succeed in doing so.

Advocacy, Self-management, Advice to Government: The Evolution of the Council of Ontario Universities

IAN CLARK

Ontario's seventeen universities devote more effort to collective endeavour than do universities in most other jurisdictions in North America. They do this through the Council of Ontario Universities (COU). The council's three primary functions are *advocacy* (advancing the cause of higher education both publicly and with the provincial government); *self-management* (providing common services, promoting best practices, undertaking quality appraisals, and occasionally dealing with issues of resource allocation among member institutions); and providing *advice to government* (often through jointly staffed committees).

The role of COU has been influenced by a number of trends and pressures that affect governments and universities in other jurisdictions. These include: the growing conviction that a jurisdiction's economic prospects are linked to the education of its population and to the research activities of its institutions; increasing competition for government funding; emergence of new technologies; and growing demands for better systems of ensuring accountability and measuring performance. In addition, three recent developments in Ontario have affected the relationship between COU and the provincial government: the wind-up of a forty-year-old "buffer body" in 1996; the coming into force of the Ontario Lobbyists Registration Act in 1999; and the need to expand university capacity to meet dramatic increases in enrolment projected for 2003–10.[1]

I describe below how these developments have affected COU's work and, where appropriate, compare the situation in Ontario with that of publicly supported higher education elsewhere in North America. I look in turn at the framework of university education, at the emergence and roles of COU, at its advocacy, at its self-management, and at its advisory role vis-à-vis government. I also offer a brief comparison of legislation on lobbyists' registration in Canada and the United States and explain why the Ontario act does not classify COU as a lobbyist, notwithstanding COU's increasing efforts to advance higher education within government.

THE REGULATORY AND FUNDING FRAMEWORK

Provincial and Federal Roles

In the Canadian federation, provincial governments have jurisdiction over education. Virtually all universities in Canada are public, not-for-profit institutions established by acts of the provincial legislatures. Provincial governments provide the bulk of the universities' revenues[2] and, through their ministries of education or equivalent bodies, establish the conditions for the expenditure of these funds and the maximum tuition that can be charged.[3]

The federal government is involved in postsecondary education through three principal avenues: bloc transfers to the provinces; student assistance programs; and peer-adjudicated research funding from its research granting councils – the Medical Research Council (MRC), the Natural Sciences and Engineering Research Council (NSERC), and the Social Sciences and Humanities Research Council (SSHRC).

The federal government has recently created two new arm's-length institutions – the Canada Foundation for Innovation (1997) to fund capital infrastructure through a peer-adjudicated process based primarily on research merit, and the Canadian Millennium Scholarship Foundation (1998), to supplement the integrated federal and provincial programs of student assistance through arrangements with provincial governments. In 1999 Ottawa announced its intention to fund up to two thousand "21st Century Chairs for Research Excellence," through the granting councils, in a manner that is related to each university's success in the peer-adjudicated grant process. Although the federal government is a major source of funds, it exerts no direct regulatory authority over the operations of Canadian universities.

Ontario and Its Universities

Ontario is Canada's most populous province, with 11.4 million people. It has a higher percentage of people aged 18 to 25 years enrolled in universities and community colleges than most other jurisdictions in North America.[4]

Each university has been established through its own act of the legislature,[5] which provides it with its own governing body. The provincial government appoints some members of the governing bodies of most, but not all, universities.[6] Through the Degree Granting Act, the province can prevent any institution from delivering educational services towards the granting of a degree. Apart from a small denominational institution, the seventeen members of COU are the only institutions based in Ontario that offer degrees and are the only degree-granting institutions that receive a provincial grant.

Provincial Funding

The bulk of provincial funding takes the form of an operating grant based on a negotiated overall level of activity measured by program-weighted, full-time equivalent enrolment ("basic income units"). Provided that the three-year average of these units stays within a "corridor" of 3 per cent above or below the negotiated level, the university is free to set its enrolment and program mix knowing that its operating grant will not be affected.[7] Each university receives annually a modest allotment for capital renewal, based on its share of calculated requirements for space. Government contributions to major capital projects are negotiated case by case with the ministry.

Ontario universities believe that the funding mechanism is well suited to the task. Indeed, they have reviewed this matter at length within COU and have not found an alternative mechanisms in any another jurisdiction that they would prefer. This satisfaction does not extend to the level of funding. Ontario's 15 per cent reductions in government grants in 1995–96 were among the most severe university cutbacks in any OECD jurisdiction. Ontario's universities are among Canada's least well funded in terms of provincial funds per capita or per student; recent trends in funding have been far less favourable than those in most U.S. states.[8]

Regulatory Regime

Ontario universities are among the most autonomous of publicly assisted universities in North America.

Although the "regulatory burden" imposed by the provincial government is greater than university administrators would like, it is focused on from issues: verification of enrolment numbers used to calculate the university's position in its "corridor"; submissions and reporting for the limited – but growing – number of "targeted programs"; information on tuition and related fee schedules; and submissions and reporting related to capital grants. Each year universities file projected and audited financial statements. Like most governments, the province encourages organizations receiving public funds to publish "performance measures." The first such mandated measures appeared in May 1999. Each university was obliged to place on its web site the results of a ministry-approved survey of graduation rates and employment rates by program (with twenty-six standard program areas defined), as well as rates of defaults in student loans, as determined by the ministry.

University–College Relationships

Community colleges in Canada have a more applied vocational mandate than the typical American junior college. In most provinces they do not serve primarily as feeder institutions into the upper years of university, although many have well-developed articulation and collaboration agreements. For the most part, community colleges in Ontario give diplomas, and universities, degrees. Although almost all of Canada's community colleges are publicly funded and regulated, many private, for-profit "career colleges" and "vocational schools" provide training and various non-degree credentials.

The university–college distinction in Ontario is among the sharpest in Canada: only universities can grant degrees; there is still relatively little movement of students between the two systems;[9] and there are no "university colleges" or "polytechnics" that combine the missions of both institutions.[10]

Universities and colleges in Ontario are placing increased priority on designing ways to better enable students to move between the sectors. Many are designing collaborative joint programs from which students can emerge with both a college diploma and a university degree. COU has actively supported these initiatives and has worked with the college association to improve system-wide opportunities for articulation. In 1999 COU and the Association of Colleges of Applied Arts and Technology of Ontario signed the Ontario Degree Completion Accord.

COLLECTIVE ENDEAVOUR THROUGH THE COUNCIL OF ONTARIO UNIVERSITIES

COU's Origins and Objects

The Committee of Presidents of the Universities of Ontario was established in 1962 and was reconstituted as the Council of Ontario Universities in 1971.[11] From the beginning, membership has consisted of all the institutions classified as universities by the province. The number has grown from ten[12] in the early 1960s to seventeen after passage of the acts creating Ryerson Polytechnic University and Nipissing University in the early 1990s.

COU's constitution states that its objects are "to promote cooperation among the provincially assisted universities, and between them and the Government of the Province, and, generally, to work for the improvement of higher education for the people of Ontario." This general mandate is comparable to that of many other province- or state-level associations[13] in jurisdictions that have more than one publicly assisted university but where the universities are not bound by formal relationships such as those between the constituent parts of the University of California system.

The Challenge of Self-management

During the 1960s – a period of rapid university expansion to meet the requirements of the "baby boom" – Ontario's university presidents deliberated at length on the nature of their newly formed association.[14] They recognized that in the United States, the general view was that "purely voluntary methods of coordination are no longer effective, and voluntary agencies are being superseded by those with statutory status and authority."[15] Nevertheless they were motivated by the straightforward challenge set out by Minister for University Affairs (later premier) William G. Davis:

There is, moreover, much evidence to indicate that provided the universities can meet the responsibilities of our times we should undoubtedly be better off if they were allowed to operate with ... autonomy. On the other hand, if they cannot or will not accept those responsibilities, and if, for example, large numbers of able students ·must be turned away because the university is not prepared to accept them, or if, as another example, some of the less glamorous disciplines are ignored despite pressing demands for graduates in those areas, or if costly duplication of effort is evident, I cannot imagine that any society will want to stand idly by. For there will inevitably be a demand – there have been indications of this in other jurisdictions – that government move in and take over.[16]

While the university presidents recognized the difficulties inherent in undertaking collective endeavours that could affect "system planning" and allocation of resources among member institutions, they saw such efforts as a means of preserving autonomy. There is little doubt that subsequent governments shared Davis's conception of self-management. Universities continue to recognize the likely link between their long-term autonomy and their acting in ways that meet both their institutional and their collective responsibilities.

University Commitment and Staff Resources

Ontario's universities undertake more common services and self-regulation collectively than their counterparts in most other jurisdictions. They use a common timetable for applications and oversee a centre that processes almost all undergraduate applications to the seventeen universities. There is a self-regulated process for approval and quality assurance for all graduate programs. Exchange agreements link all university libraries, and an inter-university transit system carries mail, documents, and library materials. There are common standards for financial reporting and collection of statistics. Numerous consortium arrangements cover purchasing and provision of information to schools and the public. Each year the universities take common "COU positions" to government on a wide variety of rather detailed program and funding issues.

These impressive results have required a commitment to collective action that is probably greater than that in most other jurisdictions. The universities pay the total costs of COU, with its thirty employees and $3-million annual budget.[17] Most university presidents are active in COU. In recent times, the chair of council[18] has been in almost daily contact with COU's president and senior staff members during much of the year. University presidents typically devote from six to fifteen day-equivalents per year to COU meetings.[19]

COU Affiliate Bodies

There are twenty-five organizations affiliated to COU, many provided with secretariat support from COU staff. These include organizations of vice-presidents, administration; vice-presidents, research; vice-presidents, academic; deans of medicine; deans of law; deans of engineering; deans of arts and science; registrars; directors of public affairs; and directors of institutional analysis. These groups have objectives similar to parallel ones in many other jurisdictions – to share experiences and compare practices. Many of the groups in Ontario meet monthly and believe that they have more extensive collective activities than their counterparts elsewhere.

One affiliate, the Ontario Council on Graduate Studies, is particularly noteworthy. This is the body, comprising the seventeen deans of graduate studies, that oversees the appraisal process for all proposed and existing graduate programs. The work is undertaken by three appraisal committees and by independent consultants engaged for each review. Ontario's process for reviewing graduate programs is recognized as a North American leader in comprehensiveness and rigour. The government has in effect established successful appraisal as a requirement for funding.

The Ontario Council on University Affairs (OCUA), 1958–96

The OCUA (and its predecessor entities) operated from 1958 to 1996. It was created by the government to have an advisory rather than a decision-making role. OCUA concentrated on system and allocation issues and was not a formal accreditation body.[20] Edward Monahan, a former executive director of the COU, has recently described[21] the various unsuccessful attempts during the 1960s and 1970s to give the OCUA the kind of planning and decision-making authority exercised by the Universities Grants Committee in Britain. Monahan attributes failure both to the universities, which, through COU, consistently resisted constraints on their autonomy, and to the government, which proved less than enthusiastic about strengthening the planning capacity and decision-making authority of an arm's-length body.

Monahan characterizes OCUA as gradually losing its effectiveness after the 1970s, so that by the mid-1990s the universities saw it as too much an instrument of government, and the government viewed it as ineffective. In 1996 the OCUA was wound up as part of a government-wide drive to reduce the number and cost of its agencies. Monahan considers the OCUA's demise a lost opportunity for better system planning and believes that its disappearance will inevitably affect the "delicate balance between university autonomy and government control in ways that are harmful both to the universities and to the society they serve."[22] To this point, at least, neither the universities nor the government have expressed support for this view.

ADVOCACY

Public and Governmental Advocacy

The advocacy function – "to work for the improvement of higher education for the people of Ontario" – has always been an essential part of COU's mission. Universities expect that one of the results of such work will be greater public funding.

COU communicates with the public through the same mechanisms employed by other sector associations: publications, press releases, media relations, press interviews, presentations, and speeches by staff and members. This work is co-ordinated through COU's Committee on Government and Community Relations and through the Ontario University Public Affairs Council – the COU affiliate on which the directors of public affairs of all seventeen universities sit.

COU is strictly non-partisan and does not endorse or financially contribute to political parties. COU deals with government, primarily through established channels with ministers and their public servants.

Registration of Lobbyists

COU advocates the interests of higher education to the public and the government. COU is clearly an advocate; but is it a lobbyist? In 1999 the government proclaimed the Lobbyists Registration Act, which required all associations and institutions in Ontario to make this determination. Each university and COU had to ascertain whether it was a lobbyist for the purposes of the act. This led to a careful review of how COU relates to government. The conclusion reached was that neither COU nor any of the universities qualified as lobbyists. The results of this review are described in a letter to Ontario's integrity commissioner – the newly created office to oversee the Lobbyists Registration Act.[23]

Such legislation was, until the 1980s, primarily an American phenomenon. Congress considered legislative proposals to regulate lobbying activity for almost a century before passing the first law in 1946. By the mid-1990s, all fifty states required lobbyists to register.[24] In Canada, Parliament passed the first such act in 1989 and amended it in 1995.[25] Ontario is the only province to have followed suit, passing its legislation, modelled closely on the amended federal statute, in 1998, with most provisions coming into force in 1999. There is no comparable legislation in Britain,[26] Scandinavia,[27] or Japan.[28] Australia introduced registration in 1984 but abolished it in 1996.[29]

These differences in legislative treatment of lobbying derive at least in part from differences in government structure. American jurisdictions work with a sharper separation of powers between the legislature and the executive than parliamentary systems, and the focus of most U.S. legislation has been the legislature. In parliamentary governments, the chief locus of decision-making and legislative initiative is the minister (in the context of cabinet government), supported by civil service advisers. Few if any significant legislative or budgetary initiatives in Ontario or other Canadian governments come from legislators other than ministers. To illustrate the difference, some U.S. states require registration of any members of the executive who deal with the legislature – a proposition that would be inconceivable in parliamentary governments.

Legislation typically requires lobbyists to register so that the client, the area of interest, and usually the organization lobbied become part of the public record. Such a system requires definitions for the terms "lobbying" and "lobbyist" and minimum thresholds of such activity.

The provisions in the Ontario legislation are typical:

Lobbying occurs when a paid lobbyist communicates with a public office holder in an attempt to influence:

- the development of any legislative proposal by any member of the Legislative Assembly;
- the introduction, passage, defeat or amendment of any bill or resolution;
- the making or amendment of any regulation;
- the development, amendment or termination of any policy or program;
- any decision about privatization or outsourcing;
- the awarding of any grant, contribution or other financial benefit by or on behalf of the Crown.

It defines "consultant lobbyist" and "organization lobbyist." The latter is "an individual who is employed by an organization, a significant part of whose duties is to lobby on behalf of the organization, or a part of whose duties is to lobby on behalf of the organization, if these duties together with the lobbying duties of other employees would constitute a significant part of the duties of one employee."

While the act makes no specific reference to universities, the guidelines to New York's law specifically mention universities (colleges).[30]

Ontario and Canadian regulations define "significant part" to be more than 20 per cent of a person-equivalent's time during any three-month period. American regimes frequently define the threshold in terms of a dollar amount of expenditures in a year – for example, $5,000 in California.

The exceptions to the act suggest the different relationship between government and lobbyists in the two countries. The following activities are not considered lobbying in Ontario:

communications that are purely consultative and essential to public policy making are not lobbying. More specifically, lobbying does not include:

- oral or written submissions to a committee of the Legislative Assembly which are a matter of public record;
- oral or written submissions made to a public office holder about enforcing, interpreting or applying any act or regulation by that public office holder;

- oral or written submissions made to a public office holder about implementing or administering any policy, program, directive or guideline by that public office holder;
- oral or written submissions in direct response to written requests for advice or comment.

In the United States, most acts do not have such exceptions.

The main reason that COU and its member institutions do not qualify as lobbyists has to do with the nature of the contact with government, not with the extent of the contact. Most interactions take the form of joint committees and responses to requests from the government. In other words, the function is that of "advisor" or "stakeholder" rather than "lobbyist." Thus, although COU consistently advocates the collective interests of Ontario's universities, both publicly and in government, it is not a lobbyist as defined by federal and Ontario legislation.

SELF-MANAGEMENT

Ontario universities have developed a long list of self-management initiatives over the years and devote considerable resources to sustaining and improving them. This quest for institutional autonomy has led to the demise of "buffer bodies."

The wind-up of OCUA, coupled with substantial staffing reductions within the Ministry of Education and Training,[31] has placed additional demands on COU to take on analytical and consensus-developing functions. Some of these tasks can affect the allocation of government grants among COU's members.

Given the different mission, size, and program focus among the seventeen universities, most funding initiatives have differential impacts. Two recent examples illustrate the point.

First, in May 1998 the government announced a program of financial incentives for institutions that could produce a credible plan for "doubling the pipeline" of places in computer science and electrical engineering within five years. The program's attractiveness to a university would depend on the institution's existing mission and concentration in these programs, as well as on such design parameters as definition of base year, definition of eligible programs, and treatment of graduate programs. Working with COU, the government refined the design parameters, including allowing a less-than-doubling expansion at the University of Waterloo, Canada's best-known computer science institution, in such a way that all universities could participate in the initiative.

Second, in early 1999, the government consulted with universities on the best way to increase enrolment in teacher education in 1999–2000. COU produced a consensus position on target enrolment increases for each institution and the amount of funding per student. Following informal undertakings from the ministry, the institutions were able to issue offers of admission to students in March 1999, two months before the government was able to make formal commitments of funds in the context of its annual budget-determination process.

I now attempt to generalize from these examples and to classify the types of issues that come to COU for consideration. (The two cases just cited would be classified as type 2.)

- type 1: positive sum with equitable distribution – for example increased operating grant; decreased government regulation
- type 2: positive sum without losers – for example, targeted spending programs with new money
- type 3: positive sum with potential losers – for example, reduction in or restriction on number of institutions offering programs in particular disciplines
- type 4: constant sum – for example, change in grant formula without new money

As expected, it has proven relatively easy to secure consensus on type-1 issues. It is not as easy to develop consensus on type 2, but as our two cases above illustrate, it is possible. Type-2 issues become much harder to deal with if institutions view success in relative terms, where any gain proportionately less than that of competitors seems a loss. Type-3 issues, where some institutions suffer an absolute loss, are notoriously difficult for voluntary associations. The logic of collective action suggests that the way to secure agreement is by bundling type-3 issues with other issues or through side payments to the losers, so that each institution can secure a net gain. Such bundling, or linking, can take place at a particular time, or over time, so that a university could take a present loss "for future considerations" and a net gain over the longer term.

An example of bundling appears in COU's 1997 declaration of unanimous support for the "directions" enunciated in the government-commissioned *Report of the Advisory Panel for Future Directions in Post-secondary Education* as a "framework for public policy" and urging the government to work with COU towards rapid implementation. The report contained many recommendations, some of which (such as encouragement of more flexibility and differentiation in tuition fees) were contrary to the previously expressed positions of some universities. Nevertheless, each COU member believed that the over-all package of recommendations would be of net benefit and that there would be a higher probability of securing this benefit if the universities were united in their general support of the report.

COU has been successful in developing consensus in type-2 issues and in bundling some potential type-3 issues in a package that could achieve consensus. However, it is obviously a continuing challenge to frame and enforce such decisions in a voluntary association. Indeed, development of consensus on issues that substantially affect inter-university allocation is a task ill-suited to a membership-based organization. But in the absence of a "buffer body," Ontario university presidents can:

- remain aloof and have the government take decisions without advice from universities
- encourage the government to make decisions based on individual submissions from seventeen universities
- attempt to present the government with a COU consensus position

To date, university presidents have usually preferred to develop a collective view whenever consensus seems remotely possible.

ADVICE TO GOVERNMENT

Ontario is projected to have by far the greatest increase in university enrolment of any Canadian province in the period 2003–10. This is a result of demography (Ontario's 18–24 cohort will be growing more rapidly than that of most other provinces) and of the government's secondary school reform that will reduce the number of high school years from five to four (so that in 2003 there will be a "double cohort" of graduates entering university).

For forty years governments of all political stripes have sought to "provide a university place for all willing and qualified students," and the universities have always been able to do so. The projections suggest a required increase of 30 to 40 per cent in system capacity – a powerful incentive for government and universities to work together to meet this challenge.

CONCLUSIONS

Across the range of funding and governance factors, Ontario appears to be near the extremes of the scale relative to other North American jurisdictions on several attributes. Ontario is, for example, at the high end for participation rates in postsecondary institutions, for university autonomy, for self-regulation, for tuition levels, and for projected increases in enrolment. It is at the low end for per-student funding and for government regulation.

One might speculate whether some of these features are linked. One could argue that the universities' extensive efforts at collective self-regulation have permitted the government to allow more institutional autonomy with less regulation than would otherwise have been the case. Similarly, extensive collaboration on administrative issues and sharing of practices has produced system efficiencies that have allowed lower government operating grants. But the universities believe that the relatively high rates of postsecondary participation and the system efficiencies do not provide a convincing reason for the comparatively low level of per-student funding in Canada's wealthiest province. The low funding creates a continuing challenge for COU's advocacy function.

On most issues, COU members have concluded that their advocacy is more effective if the actions of individual members are co-ordinated. Similarly, they believe that their advice to government will be more useful if COU is capable of ensuring reliable and comparable data and if the analysis benefits from an orderly consideration of all the relevant institutional factors. Thus for both the advocacy and the advisory functions there is an ongoing incentive for members to co-operate.

The incentives for collective action are less clear for self-management, at least for those elements affecting resource allocation. Is it desirable or feasible for a voluntary association such as COU to take on any of the functions of inter-member allocation formerly conducted by a government-appointed body? Its main incentives to do so are to provide a service that the government finds useful (and thereby enhance the credibility of its advocacy and of its self-regulatory and advisory functions) and to avoid a worse alternative.

Designating some entity as a buffer is useful for governments anxious to keep allocative decisions out of a political forum, where the media can create perceived losers. Governments in Ontario, as elsewhere, often prefer a less rancorous arbiter, such as "a neutral third party," "a well-established formula," or "consensus among the stakeholders." Since a formal third party is not currently available in Ontario, the government will tend to rely on formulae and to encourage the universities to generate a consensus.

Universities also usually prefer a consensus approach, since resolution through a highly political process may be costly in time and risky in outcome. There has been enough incentive for cou to take on – albeit with trepidation – some of the allocative functions formerly conducted by the Ontario Council on University Affairs.

The three functions – advocacy, self-management, advice – are interrelated, and cou's approach to each tries to take account of the impact on the other two. The relation between the advocacy and advisory functions is perhaps the most delicate. In recent times, cou has made a concerted effort to strengthen its working relationship with the government. Although cou's mandate obliges it to make public its analyses of the effects of government policy on higher education, it usually employs less hard-hitting language than do student and faculty associations when drawing attention to fiscal parsimony or regulatory zeal.

Although maintaining an appropriate relationship among the three functions requires continuing judgments, the functions are in many ways mutually reinforcing. Better self-management increases credibility in advisory and advocacy functions. All three require a common base of excellent data and analysis. cou improves its performance as advocate, as self-manager, and as adviser by having the most reliable and current data and by being able to understand and present their implications. cou has traditionally devoted the bulk of its staff resources to data collection and analysis. The recent experience with cou–government working groups has reinforced this trend, and now the bulk of cou's budget for external contract goes to this activity.

The generic challenges of collective decision-making in a voluntary association that Ontario's university presidents identified in the 1960s have not diminished. One might even expect them to grow as competition continues to increase for top professors, good students, government funds, and private donations. However, we saw above the continuing incentives for universities to work together in advocacy, self-management, and advice to government. As they face the challenges of collective endeavour in the new millennium, Ontario's universities can find reassurance in the solid accomplishments, consensus-making infrastructure, and personal trust produced by four decades of active co-operation.

NOTES

1 This priority is reflected in the designation, following the government's re-election in June 1999, of a Ministry of Training, Colleges and Universities.

2 In 1997–98 59 per cent of the operating revenues of Ontario universities came from the provincial government, 33 per cent from tuition fees, and 8 per cent from investment income, sales, and the like. Although the portion of operating revenues coming from government has been declining over the years (from 80 per cent in the 1970s) and is lower than that in most other provinces, it still provides over 50 per cent of revenue in all but one university.

3 Ontario has provided more tuition flexibility in fees than other provincial governments. Most professional and certain other high-demand programs are now "tuition deregulated." Tuition fees for programs where the maximum is still regulated (such as undergraduate arts and science, where annual fees average about $3,500 in 1998–99) are higher than those in other provinces, except Nova Scotia, where the government has traditionally not regulated fees. Tuition fees for these programs in Ontario are roughly comparable, in terms of purchasing power, to those of public universities in many U.S. states.

4 Ontario's participation rates in 1998–99 stood at 21.9 per cent for universities and 13.2 per cent for colleges (based on the percentage enrolled as full-time students), and early indications were that rates would rise above 22 per cent in 1999–2000. Based on data from 1996–97, Ontario ranked fourth among provinces for university participation and third for postsecondary education as a whole. For people 18–21 and 22–25 years old, Canada's postsecondary participation rates are considerably higher than those in most of the twenty-eight other OECD countries. For those 18–21, in 1996, Canada's rates were 23.1 per cent for universities and 40.5 per cent for total postsecondary, compared to U.S. figures of 21.7 per cent and 34.6 per cent, respectively, and OECD

averages of 15.2 per cent and 23.2 per cent. For those 22–25, Canada's rates were 14.6 per cent for universities and 21.9 per cent for total post-secondary – again higher than the U.S. figures of 14.0 per cent and 21.5 per cent, respectively, and the OECD averages of 13.0 per cent and 16.9 per cent.

5 Queen's has a royal charter of 1841 rather than an enabling provincial statute.

6 For example, the government appoints fifteen of the fifty members of the University of Toronto's governing council, four of twenty-seven members of the board of governors of the University of Western Ontario, but none of the members of the boards of Brock, Carleton, Queen's, Trent, or York.

7 In practice, when universities have had enrolments in excess of 3 per cent of their corridor mid-point, they have been permitted to keep the full additional value of the tuition fees but have not had their operating grant increased. In addition to the basic operating grant, there have been occasional special incentive programs to encourage universities to increase enrolment in program areas deemed of high priority by the government. A 1998 program doubled enrolment in computer science and high-demand engineering programs.

8 Ontario government funding for universities is lowest of any province on a per capita basis and second lowest per student. Compared to public universities in major American states, Ontario's research and doctoral-level universities had approximately 30 per cent less total operating revenue per student, based on 1995–96 data. Between 1995–96 and 1998–99, U.S. states' support for postsecondary education *increased* by an average of 19 per cent, while in Ontario provincial support *declined* by 11 per cent.

9 Approximately 8 per cent of university applicants have previously attended an Ontario community college.

10 Although Ryerson Polytechnic University has both "polytechnic" and "university" in its name, the institutional emphasis is very much on the latter.

11 By 1967 the practice had been established for each president to be accompanied at committee by an academic colleague. Academic colleagues became formal members of council when the Committee of Presidents of Universities of Ontario became the COU in 1971.

12 Carleton, Guelph, McMaster, Ottawa, Queen's, Toronto, Waterloo, Western Ontario, Windsor, and York.

13 Canadian universities are represented nationally by the Association of Universities and Colleges of Canada (AUCC). The colleges have the

Association of Canadian Community Colleges. Although the mandates of both national organizations include liaison with the federal government, the relationship to each level of government differs because of the respective areas of jurisdiction – the federal government has no branch of government responsible for universities and colleges. In Ontario, the twenty-five community colleges are represented by the Association of Colleges of Applied Arts and Technology of Ontario.

14 See particularly the first and second annual reviews of the Committee of Presidents of Universities of Ontario. Their titles provide a sense of the major themes of the day: *System Emerging* (1967) and *Collective Autonomy* (1968).

15 Thomas R. McConnell, "Governments and the University: A Comparative Analysis," in *Governments and the University* (Toronto: Macmillan, 1966), 83. This reference was cited in the second annual review, noted above.

16 William G. Davis, "The Government of Ontario and the Universities of the Province," in *Governments and the University* (Toronto: Macmillan, 1966), 34.

17 This does not include the thirty-five staff members and $6-million annual budget of the Ontario Universities Application Centre, which reports to COU through the president of COU. The centre is funded from application fees.

18 The chair from July 1997 to September 1999 was J. Robert S. Prichard, president of the University of Toronto. He was succeeded by Paul Davenport, president of Western Ontario, in September 1999. Chairs typically serve two years. Council selects the president for a five-year term. The two immediate previous COU presidents, Peter George and Bonnie Paterson, are currently presidents of McMaster and Trent, respectively.

19 In addition to the afternoon–evening–morning meetings associated with the five regular meetings of council, there are many committees and task forces and meetings with senior government officials. Participation in these activities varies among members. There are generally relatively few absences at regularly scheduled meetings.

20 The universities' self-regulatory body for graduate studies, the Ontario Council of Graduate Studies, formerly reported its reviews to OCUA.

21 Edward J. Monahan, "University–Government Relations in Ontario: The History of a Buffer Body, 1958–1996," *Minerva* 36 (1998), 347–66.

22 Ibid., 36.

23 Letter of 20 April 1999 from the President of the Council of Ontario Universities to The Honourable Robert C. Rutherford, Integrity

Commissioner. This letter is a public document, available from the Office of the Integrity Commissioner or cou, both in Toronto.

24 Clive S. Thomas, "Interest Group Regulation across the United States: Rationale, Development and Consequences," *Parliamentary Affairs* (Oct. 1998), 500(l).

25 Michael Rush, "The Canadian Experience: The Lobbyists Registration Act," ibid., 516(l).

26 Grant Jordan, "Towards Regulation in the UK: From 'General Good Sense' to 'Formalised Rules,'" ibid., 524(l).

27 Rene E. Rechtman, Larsen Ledet, and Jesper Panum, "Regulation of Lobbyists in Scandinavia: A Danish Perspective," ibid., 579(l).

28 Ronald J. Hrebenar, Akira Nakainura, and Akio Nakamura, "Lobby Regulation in the Japanese Diet," ibid., 551(1).

29 John Warhurst, "Locating the Target: Regulating Lobbying in Australia," ibid., 538(l).

30 "Any officer, director, trustee, employee, counsel, or agent of the State of New York who lobbies on behalf of same, when discharging his or her official duties [is not required to register]; however, an officer, director, trustee, employee, counsel, or agent of a college, as defined by Section 2 of the Education Law, must register if he or she meets the requirements of the Act."

31 In 1999 the Universities Branch of the Ministry of Training, Colleges and Universities (not including the Student Support Branch, the immediate office staff of the assistant deputy minister for post-secondary education, or the deputy minister and minister) had twenty-nine employees, almost the same number as cou.

Human Rights in Europe: Effects on Governance of British Universities

MICHAEL J. BELOFF

In this chapter I discuss the possible impact of Britain's Human Rights Act, 1998 (HRA), on universities[1] in England and Wales in terms of its incorporation of the European Convention on Human Rights (ECHR),[2] effective 2 October 2000. The legislation had a two-year incubation period. Like the Olympic long jump, it had an extensive run-up followed by a leap into the unknown, although Scotland had used the ECHR as a measuring rod for legislation and executive acts for one year.

This trial run in Scotland revealed the wide-ranging effect that the domesticated ECHR will have not only on the substance of law, but also on the identity of those who apply it.[3] In one case a court ruled that the system of part-time sheriffs (PTSs) contravened article 6, which requires an independent and impartial judiciary as an element of a fair trial. Since, in criminal matters, a Scottish government officer acts as prosecutor but also helps appoint the PTS, the PTS might favour the prosecution in hope of preferment. In another case, a court disqualified a senior judge who in a series of newspaper articles had described the ECHR as a "Trojan horse" – his most favourable comment – on grounds of predisposition from sitting on a case that involved its application. No doubt the court *thought* of what Prime Minister Atlee once *said* to a voluble colleague: "A period of silence from you would be most welcome." There are even concerns that the lord chancellor (LC), being a member of the executive, a legislator, and a judge, may have to shed some powers in light of the theory of the separation of powers.[4]

I first outline the structure of the HRA; second, analyse its application to education; and third, describe some of the other provisions in the HRA that may influence education law. The HRA's object is to depart from the traditional common law concept of negative liberties – doing what is not forbidden – and to bring into English law a positive statement of rights – doing what is permitted. These rights are in essence entitlements, which people can assert against a public authority who has, as the case may be, either breached them or failed properly to protect them.[5] Whether the rights have a horizontal effect – i.e., between private persons, natural or legal – in addition to a vertical effect – i.e., between private persons and public authorities – is a matter of great academic controversy.

STRUCTURE OF THE HUMAN RIGHTS ACT (HRA)

The core provisions of the HRA are sections 2, 3, and 6–8. Section 6 makes it unlawful for a public authority to act in a way that is incompatible with a convention right, unless a statutory provision that cannot be read in a manner that is compatible with it positively requires it to do so.[6] This exception ought to be triggered rarely, since section 3 renders statutory provisions usually capable of a meaning compatible with the convention, even if under a somewhat strained meaning.

Section 3 of the HRA requires that interpretation of all legislation, primary or secondary, whether enacted before or after the HRA, conform with the convention "wherever possible." However, the HRA cannot be used to invalidate primary legislation. As such it differs in its potency from, for example, the U.S. Constitution and its Bill of Rights.

In short, sections 6 and 3 (read together) impose a new general statutory duty on public authorities to act in compliance with the convention.

In determining any question that involves a convention claim, courts must, by virtue of section 2 of the HRA, "have regard" to the principles set out in convention case law. But the ECHR level of protection is a minimum standard. Nothing in the HRA inhibits national courts from offering a higher level of protection to human rights than the Strasbourg institutions (the international organs that previously policed the ECHR for British citizens), and will continue to do so if the citizen remains aggrieved by the disposal of his or her complaint in the English courts. The legal road still leads to Strasbourg: it is simply longer.

By virtue of section 7 of the HRA, "victims" of human rights violations[7] can challenge the failure of a public authority to comply with section 6 in any appropriate court or tribunal. Section 8 permits a court to award any remedy within its powers necessary to afford "just satisfaction." Such remedy could include an injunction, a declaration, a remedy at public law compelling or quashing a decision, or damages. Even a private institution, certain of whose functions are those of a "public nature," can qualify as a public authority for purposes of the HRA in its performance of those public functions.[8]

APPLICATION TO EDUCATION

Universities in the United Kingdom differ among themselves in their legal origin. Formerly, universities – and colleges – tended to be legal corporations created by royal charter issued pursuant to the royal prerogative. Such bodies accordingly had (and have) an officer known as a visitor, with sole and exclusive jurisdiction over "the internal arrangements and dealings ... within the institution." Disputes between students and such bodies thus go to the visitor, not to the courts, which have limited supervisory jurisdiction over the visitor's actions. I return to this matter below.

A few of the older universities were set up by act of Parliament.[9] At Oxford, the visitors deals with disputes between a student and a college, but not with those between a student and the university.

In my view, universities are clearly "public authorities," which fall within the HRA's definition – statutes affecting their governance, public funding, and provision of a public service.

Almost two decades ago – in my first major overseas case as a queen's counsel (QC) – I had to argue in Malaysia on behalf of the Chinese community for its right to set up a university whose students would be taught in Chinese. The Malaysian constitution required use of Bahasa, the national language, by all "public authorities."[10] I had an opinion written by a former attorney-general and head of a Cambridge college, which suggested that denial of permission to establish a Chinese university would amount to racial discrimination. The opinion, however, entirely missed the critical point on which the case was to turn, and it was as a result wrong, in the eyes of the Malaysian judiciary.

My first, instinctive reaction was that a private university was axiomatically not a public authority. The constitution's definition showed this first impression – as is so often the case in the law – to be false.

The case was appealed up to the Court of Appeal, which had four ethnic Malay judges and one Chinese judge. The result was a 4–1 majority against. Presciently, the government had just abolished appeals to the Privy Council in London, which might have offered a more dispassionate conclusion.

Whether the courts of England and Wales would now reach the same decision is almost purely academic, since only the University of Buckingham can claim any measure of independence from the state.

OTHER PROVISIONS OF
THE HUMAN RIGHTS ACT

So, on the basis that universities are public authorities,[11] how does the HRA affect them? Article 2 of protocol 1 of the convention provides: "No person shall be *denied* the right to education. In the exercise of any functions which it assumes in relation to education and teaching, the State shall respect the right of parents to ensure such education and teaching in conformity with their own religious and philosophical convictions."

Because the right not to be denied an education raises difficult political and economic choices, the United Kingdom has entered a reservation that binds domestic courts: "In view of certain provisions of the Education Acts in force in the United Kingdom, the principle affirmed in the second sentence of Article 2 is accepted by the United Kingdom only so far as it is compatible with the provision of efficient instruction and training and the avoidance of unreasonable public expenditure." The chancellor of the exchequer clearly won out over the lord chancellor.[12] But before any question arises about the reach of reservation, there is a prior issue of the reach of the article itself.

The European Court of Human Rights has decided four cases on article 2 of protocol 1 – all to do with schools, none with universities. It appears that the convention affords only limited protection to further and higher education, even though the language of the article is not confined to education at school. In *Campbell v. Cosans v. UK*[13] (a case about corporal punishment), the court described the education of children as "the whole process whereby, in any society, adults endeavour to transmit their beliefs, culture and other values to the young, whereas teaching or instruction refer in particular to the transmission of knowledge and to intellectual development."[14]

In *Belgian Linguistics* (a case about whether the Belgian government should subsidize francophone schools),[15] the commission ruled that the right to education "includes entry to nursery, primary, secondary and higher education." However, it has since drawn a distinction between elementary education, which allows universal access, and advanced studies, where individual rights may be more limited. It has held that it is *not* incompatible with the convention to restrict access to higher education to students who have attained the particular academic level required to benefit from the courses offered.[16] The English comic novelist Kingsley Amis said about university expansion: "More will mean worse." The ECHR does not at any rate compel more.

The English Court of Appeal has taken a similarly restrictive position. *O'Connor v. CEO*[17] concerned the denial of a state welfare benefit to a student. The student had failed preliminary exams and was entitled to pursue his course only as an external student, which meant that he received no student grant. The court held that the article is "concerned primarily with school, not higher education."

Moreover, it is well established that the right to education calls for regulation by the state, which may vary with the needs and resources of the community and of individuals. While such regulation must never injure the substance of the right to education or conflict with other rights enshrined in the convention, recourse to disciplinary measures, including suspension and expulsion, does not injure the substance of the right to education, provided that the affected individual may enrol elsewhere.[18]

The limitation on the levels of education affected by the article is mirrored in a limitation on the extent of that effect. In *Belgian Linguistics* (No. 2)[19] the court decided that the first sentence of article 2 of protocol 1 does enshrine a positive right, but a right with a relatively narrow content – access to available educational institutions, a right to be taught in the national language (or one of them), and a right to official recognition of qualifications obtained. By contrast, there is no right to require states to establish at their own expense, or to subsidize, education of any particular type or at any particular level – for example (in *Belgian Linguistics*), the right for individuals to be taught, at state expense, in the language of their parents' choice (in that instance, French).

The object of the second sentence of article 2 of protocol 1 is to prevent the indoctrination of children through the education system, by requiring the state to accord due respect to parents' philosophical and religious convictions. The right to "respect" for a parent's convictions (meaning views that attain a certain level of cogency, seriousness, cohesion, and importance; that are worthy of respect in a "democratic society"; and that are not incompatible with human dignity) does not mean mere acknowledgment of them or taking of them into account. It implies some positive obligations on the state, but short of creating an absolute right for a parent to have children educated in accordance with their religious or philosophical convictions.

In *Campbell v. Cosans v. UK*,[20] parents who objected on philosophical grounds to corporal punishment argued successfully that the exclusion of their child from a state school until he accepted it violated article 2 of potocol 1, on the basis that use of such punishment could be an "integral part" of the educational process. In *Kjeldsen & Others v. Denmark*,[21] Christian parents of school-age children unsuccessfully objected to compulsory sex education integrated into the curriculum of state primary schools. Parents cannot have any say in the education of those who by law, if not always by behaviour, are young adults.

But other convention articles may have an indirect, as well as a direct, impact on universities. Article 3 provides that no one shall be subject to torture or inhuman or degrading treatment. In *Campbell v. Cosans v. UK*,[22] the court rejected the argument that the existence of corporal punishment in schools was a breach of article 3, on the basis that there was no evidence that the boys in question underwent suffering of the level inherent in torture or inhuman treatment. Each case, however, will turn on its facts. In *Warwick v. UK*,[23] the caning of a sixteen-year-old girl so as to bruise her hand was held degrading, bearing in mind her age, the physical injury caused, as well as the fact that psychological injury could not be ruled out. Will universities that turn a blind eye to hazing or bullying of a kind fashionable in the U.S. fraternity houses of earlier generations be vulnerable to claims under this article?[24]

Article 8 provides a qualified right to respect for private life and correspondence, limited so far as is necessary in a democratic society for various purposes, including protection of the rights of others. A university's assertion of rights to access to e-mail for the purpose of maintaining discipline may come under review. So would any attempt to dismiss university teachers on account of their private sexual behaviour.

Article 9 provides a qualified right of freedom of thought and conscience. It is again a potential guarantor of academic freedom.

Article 10 provides a qualified right to freedom of expression and includes the right to hold opinions and also to receive and impart information and ideas without interference by public authority and regardless of frontiers, but also limited in the same way. Issues involving article 10 may also arise in relation to denial of audience to speakers who violate the precepts of political correctness, but British universities are already under a statutory duty to take such steps as may be reasonably practicable to guarantee freedom of speech within the law for members, students, and employees and for visiting speakers.[25] Article 10 issues would also surface vis-à-vis any attempt to dismiss university teachers on account of their political views.

Article 14 provides that: "The enjoyment of the rights and freedoms set forth in this Convention shall be secured without any discrimination on any ground such as sex, race, colour, language, religion, political or other opinion, national or social origin, association with a national minority, property, birth or other status."

This is not an independent anti-discrimination guarantee but forbids unjustified distinctions in application of the convention's guarantees to different persons or groups. It may therefore broaden the protection of the other convention articles if they are applied in a discriminatory way. The discrepancy in British universities between fees charged to overseas and to home (or EU) students seems an obvious target for a claim.

It has also been suggested that the HRA may also provide a remedy for students who feel that their applications to Oxford or Cambridge or other universities have not been fairly considered but have been tainted by a quota system or by class prejudice.[26]

Article 6(1) provides that, "in the determination of his civil rights and obligations, or of any criminal charge against him, everyone is entitled to a fair and public hearing within a reasonable time by an independent and impartial tribunal established by law."

The court has decided no case on whether the right not to be denied an education constitutes a "civil" right for the purposes of engaging article 6 protection or a mere public law right, and the commission, in *Simpson v. UK*,[27] has decided that it is not: likewise the English Court of Appeal in *O'Connor*.[28]

Whatever the outcome of the debate, it is likely that disciplinary decisions to exclude students (as distinct from academic decisions not to admit) made by universities may be open to successful challenge under article 6 if they do not follow fair and transparent procedures. The safeguards may need to be particularly tight if the conduct alleged may be criminal, in which case the supplemental guarantees in articles 6(2)–6(3) may be engaged.

A feature of English chartered universities as well as of colleges at Oxford and Cambridge, as I noted above, is the visitor. I was by coincidence advocate in the two major cases in this area, in both of which a university lecturer challenged a dismissal decision and was met by the argument that it was for the visitor, not the courts, to determine its propriety. In the first case, *Thomas*,[29] it was held that the visitor had exclusive jurisdiction. In the second case, *Page*,[30] it was held that the visitor's interpretation of university law was exclusive.

Only limited judicial review applies to visitors for absence of jurisdiction, abuse of power, breach of rules of natural justice, and failure to exercise judgment at all: but critically not on issues of fact or of interpretation of the domestic laws of the institution.

Concerns about the compatibility of the visitor's jurisdiction with article 6 were expressed in a recent paper by the Committee of Vice-Chancellors and Principals (CVCP) ("The Voice of the Universities," 7 June 2000).[31] The CVCP advises that "(i) Visitors should not be part of governance of institution or seem to be so; (ii) their role and functions should be made better known; (iii) process of *ad hoc* appointment should have regard to need for Visitors to be seen as independent."

CONCLUSION

As a practising queen's counsel but one whose primary interest is in Trinity College, Oxford, I cast a wistful eye at the scope for litigation that will undoubtedly arise in the years to come.

NOTES

1 See M. Hunt, in Richard McManus, *Education Law and the Courts* (London: Sweet and Maxwell, 1998), chap. 10; A. Bradley, "Scope for

Review: The Convention Right to Education and the Human Rights Act 1998," *European Human Rights Law Review* (London: Sweet and Maxwell, 1999). H. Mountfield, "The Implications of the Human Rights Act 1998 for the Law of Education," unpublished, 1999.

2 The ECHR is an international treaty to which the United Kingdom subscribed in 1950. The right of individual petition enabling British citizens to bring cases before the commission and court in Strasbourg was granted in 1967.

3 G. Anderson, *European Law Review Human Rights Survey* (2000), HR/3.

4 On invitation from the chairman, I so advised the Wakeham Commission, which reported in 1999 on the future of the House of Lords; my advice, however, was not accepted. See, however, *McGonnell v. UK* TLR 22.2 2000, involving the lesser figure of the bailiff of Guernsey.

5 M. Beloff, *What Does It All Mean? The Human Rights Act 1998*, Lasok Lecture at the University of Exeter (London: Kluer Publishers, 1999).

6 Section 6(2).

7 This definition excludes, for example, pressure groups. This is also controversial: see M. Beloff, "Who, Whom? Issues in Locus Standi," in *Essays in Honour of Lord Slynn* (London: Kluer, 2000).

8 Section 6(3)(b).

9 See for example, the Universities of Oxford and Cambridge Act, 1571; the Scottish Universities of St Andrews, Glasgow, Aberdeen and Edinburgh, Universities Act, 1858–1966; and the University of Newcastle-upon-Tyne Act, 1962.

10 *Merdeka University Berhad v. Govt. of Malaysia* 1982 MLJ 283. See M. Beloff, "Minority Languates and the Law," *Current Legal Problems* (1987).

11 A conclusion fortified by the recent case in the European Court of Justice involving the University of Cambridge. *R. v. HMT ex p. University of Cambridge* 2000 1 WLR 251.

12 Cf. Education Act, 1996, section 9, which applies the same principle in domestic statute law.

13 4 EHRR 293.

14 Para. 33.

15 1966 3 YB 56.

16 *X. v. UK* 1980 25 DR 275. *Yamasik v. Turkey* (1993) 74 DLR 14; *Sulak v. Turkey* (1996) 84 AD&R 98: see also in the Court: *Lurasch v. Russia* decision of 16/11/99.

17 1999 ELR 209.

18 1 EHRR 252.

19 1 EHRR 252.

20 4 EHRR 293.

21 EHRR 711. See also *Valsamis v. Greece* (1997 24 EHRR 294).

22 Ibid.

23 1986 60 DR 5.

24 See Mountfield, "Implications," 13, which suggests that they may be.

25 *Ex p. Caesar – Gordon* 1991, 1 QB 124.

26 R. Boyd, "Human Rights – a Game of Two Halves", *Education, Public Law and the Individual* (Oct. 2000), 13. There is no quota system at Oxford, and no class prejudice, despite the views of the chancellor of the exchequer.

27 1989 64 DR 188.

28 Ibid.

29 1987 AC 795.

30 1993 AC 682.

31 See also Dennis Farrington, "The Vistatorial Jurisdiction: A Critique and Proposals for Replacement," paper presented to Committee of Vice-Chancellors and Principals, Ontario, Canada, 7 June 2000. "The Visitatorial jurisdiction does not appear to be compatible with Article 6(1) since it denies access to ordinary courts. Appeals against the decisions of 'administrative bodies will only be consistent with Article 6(1) if they are conducted before judicial bodies with full jurisdiction.'" Tim Kaye, "Academic Judgment, the University Visitor and the Human Rights Act 1998," *Education and the Law* 11, no. 3 (1999). I am with others, reviewing the compatibility of Oxford's University and college procedures with the HRA.

Overcoming Apartheid in South African Universities: Differential Access and Excellence

DAVID R. WOODS

One of the worst features of the apartheid era in South Africa was the Nationalist government's fear of a significant, educated black middle class. To ensure that such a bloc did not develop, it spent markedly less on the education of black school children than on their white counterparts. The majority of black children have attended inferior schools, with little infrastructure, few books, and poorly qualified and unprofessional teachers. This is especially the case for mathematics, physical science, and biology. Few black school leavers have the background to succeed at university, and so South Africa faces an enormous challenge in producing the highly educated workforce needed for the twenty-first century.

The nation's universities cannot sit back and wait for the schools to be upgraded. This will take from ten to thirty years, as the school system continues to deteriorate and the number of university entrants (students with matriculation exemption) also declines from its already low levels. By way of comparison, Australia, which has a population of approximately 18 million, has about 600,000 university students (a ratio of 30:1); South Africa, with 40–45 million people, has 370,000 university students (121:1).

I look first at the recent history of the South African university system and the present context and policies. I examine next the recent experience at Rhodes University, where I work, before considering finally some ways in which South African universities can help educate more people.

HISTORY AND CONTEXT

South Africa has two major groups of universities – the historically black universities (HBUs) and the historically white ones (HWUs), which we can further subdivide into Afrikaans (HAUs) and English (HEUs). The establishment and geographical location of many of the institutions was politically motivated and had little to do with educational or human resource needs. The prime examples are universities of the apartheid-era homelands and ethnic institutions set up in areas already well served by universities.

The present funding system – the South African Post Secondary Education (SAPSE) funding formula – is based on student numbers and success rates two years earlier and hence does not facilitate planning. The formula weights the sciences and humanities in the ratio of 2.67:1. Research published in accredited journals qualifies for subsidy. The formula assumes *even* growth but makes no provision for decreasing numbers.

The SAPSE formula was instituted in the early 1980s and is calculated to cover 80 per cent of a university's cost. However, it became apparent by the mid-1980s that the government could not afford the expenditure, and so the government instituted an adjustment factor, or A-factor, to reduce funding. The A-factor in 1999 was 0.641, so that instead of the formula's funding 80 per cent of costs, it covers only 51.3 per cent. The introduction of the A-factor resulted in a rapid increase in academic fees, which reduced access for disadvantaged and indigent people. It is government policy that higher education cannot be free and that universities must charge fees, which students must pay. It is argued that graduates have access to well-paid jobs and that the state cannot afford free tertiary education.

In an attempt to facilitate access by black students, the government is funding the National Student Financial Aid Scheme. In the years from 1995 to 1999 the annual amounts made available were R55 million, R300 million, R200 million, R300 million, R390 million, respectively. The money is paid as a loan, with up to 40 per cent converted to a bursary, depending on the student's success. Unfortunately, the amount of money is inadequate and has resulted in massive fee debts, particularly at the HBUs.

The government's decision not to "bail out" universities with fee debts and its insistence that fees be paid resulted in a decrease in enrolments at HBUS in 1999. Some HBUS now have 50 per cent fewer students, with proportionally lower numbers entering university. The government's intention to "massify" university education and to increase access for blacks has received a major setback. Since SAPSE uses numbers that are two years old, the survival of these universities is uncertain, unless something is done.

As well, the SAPSE formula does not make provision for funding of academic development and support, bridging, or foundation programs. Given the inferior school system and the low numbers of matriculation exemption students, academic development and support are essential for improving access and throughput. Universities have had to find their own funds for such programs.

To overcome past inadequacies, Parliament passed the Higher Education Act in December 1997. Important features of the act include:

- establishment of a single, co-ordinated system of higher education
- promotion of co-operative governance
- program-based higher education
- representativeness and equal access
- assurance of quality
- funding based on institutions' comprehensive, strategic three-year rolling plans

Funding will consist of a block grant (the major portion, based on student places) and earmarked a redress funding (a minor portion, including academic development and capital for buildings). The details of the system are still being developed and will probably take five years to become operational.

RHODES UNIVERSITY'S EXPERIENCE

The entry of students from disadvantaged schools has had a major effect on the HWUS, which in the apartheid era had white students from a relatively uniform and advantaged school system. Perhaps the greatest challenge facing all the universities involves building capacity while at the same time ensuring excellence and enhancing exit standards.

In this section we see how Rhodes University – an HWU – has adopted differential access, differential progress, differential process, but equal exit. We also look at measures of the success of this approach.

Differential Access

Differential access is essential to facilitating entry of black students and has resulted in Rhodes University's having 48 per cent black students. This change has occurred over the last ten years. Black students who have obtained matriculation exemption, but with low marks that do not allow automatic entry, are assessed and admitted on the basis of their potential to succeed at university. The assessment involves an interview to gauge motivation and competence in English and to obtain a cognitive picture of the students. The students also complete a biographical questionnaire, which involves writing about themselves, so that their ability to express themselves in writing can be assessed.

Differential Progress

It is unrealistic to expect a black student from a disadvantaged school to complete a degree within three years. Progress is therefore slower, and completion takes four to six years, which increases costs. The university has moved away from a "bridging" year to a "foundation" year. A bridging year buffers students from university standards and leads university and academic staffers to believe, mistakenly, that students have been "brought up to speed." Foundation courses, in contrast, are embedded in the university. Students take mainstream courses while doing the foundation courses. Since the foundation courses are institutionalized, the university has to adapt to the changing student profile.

Differential Process

In the initial years of taking students from disadvantaged schools, the university established an Academic Support Programme (ASP) to assist the students. ASP involved academic support and tutorials, which we separate from academic departments and suffered accordingly. It became apparent that the university could not afford a burgeoning ASP and that having the ASP outside the departments limited its success. Furthermore, as more black students gained access, "disadvantage" would become a majority rather than a minority problem. Focusing on large numbers of historically disadvantaged students would not only be expensive but would also force students to fit into unchanged, inadequate institutions.

Hence the shift from ASP to Academic Development (AD), which concentrates on the quality of teaching and on the learning environment to which *all* students are exposed. Rhodes University set up the Academic Development Centre (ADC), where a few specialists train lecturers and transform the learning environment. To facilitate ADC's work and to improve teaching and learning in the new environment, the university has founded the Teaching and Learning Committee, which has developed policies on curriculum development and review, on evaluation of teaching and courses, and on assessment of student learning.

Equal Exit

To ensure equal exit, the university has instituted a random numbering system, as opposed to names, to identify examination scripts. All final-year courses are externally examined, and the external examiners' reports are scrutinized by the deans of the faculties. Quality-control procedures ensure regular appointment of new external examiners.

Capacity Building and Excellence

Rhodes University's approach seems to be successful, although it has increased the teaching loads of lecturers, who complain that the extra student contact is reducing their time for research. Since South Africa has only about 130 black chartered accountants, the university established the first foundation program in the commerce faculty in 1994. This program accepts and caters to apparently very weak students, who would not normally have gained access to university. Success can transform the individual student's life.

Between 1994 and 1997 the foundation program in commerce registered 100 students. To date six of its students have obtained commerce degrees, majoring in accountancy, information systems, or economics; forty-one are still studying; twenty-five were excluded after the foundation year; and a further twenty-eight "dropped out" later. In 1998 twenty-five black students were enrolled in the program. Twenty attained the minimum requirement of two academic credits. Six obtained distinctions in statistics, which is a mainstream course, and the foundation students attended lectures with the rest of the first-year commerce students.

The university's readmission policy takes into account students' backgrounds. First-time entering students from disadvantaged schools normally have two years to complete their first year of study, provided that they show commitment and academic progress. None the less, between 1993 and 1997, an average of 15.2 per cent of first-time entering black students were not readmitted after their first year at Rhodes University. The comparable figure for white students was 3.6 per cent.

We can assess the passing rates for students at Rhodes University by comparing the percentage of passes in all courses for which all students were registered. In 1996, 1997, and 1998, 81.7 per cent, 79.7 per cent, and 81.6 per cent, respectively, of all students passed. The comparable figures for black students were 77.1 per cent, 72.3 per cent, and 75.8 per cent, respectively, and for white students, 86.6 per cent, 86.9 per cent, and 87 per cent, respectively.

We can judge the success rates of black students at all universities and technikons by the result of students assisted by the National Student Financial Aid Scheme. From 1991 until 1998, 143,169 students received aid (total of R257,787). Analysis of the student cohorts for 1991, 1992, 1993, and 1994 indicates that 68 per cent, 62 per cent, 58 per cent, and 42 per cent, respectively, graduated, while 3 per cent, 7 per cent, 13 per cent, and 32 per cent, respectively, are still studying. The drop-out rates for the four years were 29 per cent, 31 per cent, 29 per cent, and 26 per cent, respectively. Students in 1995, 1996, and 1997 collectively passed 71.45 per cent, 71.6 per cent, and 75.25 per cent, respectively, of all the courses for which they registered.

EXPANDING RESEARCH CAPACITY

South African universities must also develop and maintain a research capacity. The core activities of a university are teaching and research, which are linked via the "cutting edge" principle. Good research is at the forefront of any discipline, and lecturers who are active researchers are at the "cutting edge" of their subject, which improves their teaching.

Research at a university is linked to the training of master's and doctoral students and the production of the high-level "human resources" that South Africa needs. Furthermore, transfer of complex technology and knowledge requires a research infrastructure and capacity. Original research can help South Africa's development and competitiveness.

Since the majority of domestic university research is oriented towards solving South African problems, it facilitates interaction with the wider community, which is another major aspect of a university's life. Excellence in these endeavours may result in international recognition and ease access to foreign universities and research institutes. It is a university's international passport to collaborative ventures.

The principles and strategies required for building research capacity and for achieving excellence in research are complementary, whether these activities are taking place within the same university or in different universities where the one is building capacity and the other has a record of research excellence that must be fostered and maintained. After all, success in capacity building in research will result in the ability to undertake excellent research. The two are inextricably linked and form a dynamic, cyclic combination. Research excellence provides an environment for the development of young people who in turn become excellent researchers.

Rhodes University is working to change its predominantly white staff profile and to attract capable young black students into research and academic courses. This is not easy because of the lack of skilled black people in the marketplace and the aggressive affirmative-action programs of both the private and the government sectors. Competition for capable black employees is fierce, and salaries have risen dramatically. Academic salaries are not competitive, and so the (U.S.) Mellon Foundation has provided Rhodes with funding for prestigious scholarships designed to retain and attract excellent research students. This forms part of a "growing our own timber" initiative, which has had its first notable success – appointment of a black PhD graduate in chemistry as a lecturer in pharmaceutical chemistry.

I am an advocate of group research, especially in disciplines involving laboratory, field, or community-based work. Even literature- or archival-based studies can benefit from the group approach, which can be more productive and more enjoyable, especially for postgraduate students.

In building research capacity, institutions need to move away from the "deep end" approach, which leaves academics to themselves to sink or swim. Developing researchers will require greater research funding and more industrial links and will involve offering workshops or assistance in research methods, writing research proposals, running research groups, patenting discoveries, and supervising postgraduates. An important part of a researcher's development is spending time at a leading institution overseas. Given the exchange rate of the Rand, South African academics may instead spend sabbaticals at other local universities, which would foster domestic collaboration. Given the national differential in capacities, excellent practitioners at universities with a research culture should help develop capacity at less research-oriented universities.

SUMMARY

The challenges of differential access, capacity building of black undergraduates and postgraduates, and maintaining excellence are enormous, but it is essential that we succeed. The future of South Africa depends on universities' willingness and ability to upgrade students with potential who have had to endure a disadvantaged school system. The universities cannot step back and wait decades for the school system to improve. Our success at Rhodes University encourages me, and I believe that our approaches and policies will facilitate access, build capacity, and enhance excellence.

Financing University Performance in Britain and the United States

F. KING ALEXANDER

Today, the world economy is changing economic and educational needs more rapidly than ever. Throughout the world governments are being urged to devise new strategies to adapt to a changing economic environment. The result has been a realization that to strengthen their competitive positioning states must increase their involvement in the development of human capital, research, and education. According to Marshall, "[I]n this more competitive world, dominated by knowledge-intensive technology, the keys to economic success are now human resources and not necessarily organizations of production, natural resources, and economies of scale."[1]

Colleges and universities are at the nucleus of the international movement to advance knowledge-based economies. The intellectual achievements of science and technology have clearly achieved ascendancy over the liberal education that dominated university curricula for centuries. As the *Economist* observes, "individuals with ideas, and the ability to manipulate them, count for far more than the traditional factors of production – [thus] the university has come to look like an increasingly useful asset."[2]

What has emerged from these societal developments is increased reliance on higher education to serve the economic needs of the state. Governmental organizations in the United States and other OECD nations continue to press colleges and universities to demonstrate greater efficiency and accountability in the use of public resources.

Budget reductions and general constraints on resources have become commonplace, while institutions are being asked to serve increasing numbers of students and constituencies. The traditional relationship between government and higher education is changing to better address national economic demands.

The two major sections of this essay consider the British and the American experience of the last decade or two. Some systemic comparisons and a conclusion follow. But first I look at the centuries-old struggle for accountability and control in Wastern universities.

THE LONG BATTLE FOR CONTROL

Governments' use of accountability mechanisms to balance state issues with university interests is not a recent development. History is replete with examples of governments' attempting to leverage greater control of higher education in both mind and matter. Early (medieval) requirements of accountability tended to be based largely on ecclesiastical pressures rather than on financial considerations. Disputes between institutions and government date back to the origins of Western universities in the twelfth century, when a dramatic struggle over faculty hiring and curriculum content pitted the masters at the University of Paris against the chancellor of Notre Dame Cathedral. At that time, of course, church and state were inseparable in France and throughout the continent. Years would pass before this particularly acrimonious dispute was temporarily resolved in 1231 by Pope Gregory IX, who ended the dominance of the cathedral's authorities over the university and the masters' guild.[3]

During the sixteenth and seventeenth centuries, Oxford and Cambridge were repeatedly subjected to the shifting tides of governmental upheaval and encroachment. Several acts of Parliament went so far as to prohibit the awarding of degrees to students and to remove faculty members who refused to take oaths of supremacy and obedience.[4] Accountability based on belief rather than on finance sometimes resulted in extreme governmental action, as when Henry VIII executed John Fisher, chancellor at Cambridge, who had disagreed with how the monarch resolved several issues of church and of state and, of course, Henry's personal problems.[5]

U.S. colleges and universities have experienced a steady current of external control throughout their short history. According to Lucas, criticizing higher education for Americans "has always amounted to something of a national pastime."[6] Some of the nation's most famous legal struggles involved institutional resistance to state-imposed requirements for governmentally conceived accountability. During the nineteenth century the famous Dartmouth College case helped define U.S. contract law, while the University of Michigan's highly publicized clash with the state of Michigan over institutional control ensured that state governments, like their European counterparts, would periodically demand of universities better performance and greater efficiency.

The most recent accountability movement sweeping the United States and Britain has pitted many universities that have defended traditional structures of peer review against governmental regulation premised on economic necessity. The conflict was best defined in 1990 at Westminster by the Committee of Public Accounts after its internal review of English public universities: "[W]e do not accept that their [the universities'] independence and autonomy, although undoubtedly valuable in many respects, is a valid argument against the attempts to defend against the shortcomings in realistic and effective management and control of the public funds on which universities are dependent."[7]

Despite unparalleled economic and scientific achievements attributable to higher education in the United States and Britain during the last three decades, public dissatisfaction has continued to permeate legislative halls. A spate of popular criticism has forced many institutions to re-examine their educational missions and to devise new funding alternatives in order to satisfy powerful external constituencies. These developments have placed uncommon burdens on higher education, as governments' attempt to monitor educational performance while insisting on greater efficiencies and economies of scale.

Underlying governmental demands for improved public-sector performance, "outcomes indicators" have emerged as instruments to improve institutional efficiency and effectiveness. In both the United States and Britain, performance-based systems have incorporated fiscal incentives into a new managerial framework that is forcing universities to become more productive in attaining predetermined objectives or to risk reductions in annual appropriations.

Many performance-based planning and funding initiatives have produced systems where governments regularly compare and rank the productivity of institutions. In Britain, "League Tables," similar to the ranking systems used in national football leagues, regularly compare university productivity in teaching and research.[8] In Colorado, annual report cards compare universities' effectiveness and productivity. Now national report cards compare the institutional effectiveness of U.S. states' systems of higher education.[9] To explain the evolution of many such government-devised performance-based policy reforms, this chapter discusses their development in Britain and the United States and their impact on higher education.

BRITAIN'S PERFORMANCE-BASED REFORMS

Among the numerous performance-based reforms of higher education to emerge during the last decade, the most comprehensive and notable policies have emerged in Britain. In response to the increased drive for greater accountability, British universities have witnessed unprecedented intervention by the central government into their governance and fiscal affairs. Partington refers to this encroachment as a direct "legacy of Thatcherism" and the priorities that were part of the conservative Tory philosophy.[10] Its main vehicles, examined below, are research assessment exercises (RAES); the Higher Education Funding Councils (HEFCS) for England, Scotland, and Wales; and teaching quality assessments (TQAS).

Research Assessment Exercises (RAES)

During the last decade and a half, the relationship between Parliament and higher education has changed almost beyond recognition. Performance-based policy first surfaced in 1985 when the University Grants Committee (UGC) concluded that quality of research, unlike that of teaching, can be quantified. It devised the first research assessment exercise (RAE) to assess and compare the quality of institutions' and departments' research.[11]

After the initial RAE in the mid-1980s, Parliament passed the Education Reform Act of 1988. The act facilitated the eventual centralization of fiscal authority and control in Parliament, while also mandating that higher education double its enrolment by the turn of the century. Government would not offer corresponding financial support for such changes. Structurally, the act eliminated the UGC, once perceived as a buffer, or mediating institution, between central government and institutions. The Thatcher government saw the UGC as a defender of waste and of vested interests and as representing traditional university values.[12] The act also made all polytechnic institutions independent from the powerful local education authorities (LEAS).

In 1991 a government white paper proposed substantial changes in the system – most notably, abolition of the "binary line" between the universities and the polytechnics and colleges. A new unitary system of higher education had definitive funding ties to the national government, creating a more competitive funding environment for universities.

Higher Education Funding Councils (HEFCS)

The Further and Higher Education Act (1992) established separate funding councils for England (HEFCE), Scotland (SHEFC), and Wales (HEFCW), effectively transferring a significant portion of funding authority from the UGC and the LEAS to the central government.[13] HEFCS transformed higher education by centralizing state authority. The original mission of the HEFCS was to promote the quality and quantity of learning and to foster increased research. The government wanted greater cost effectiveness in a system perceived as moribund and as unresponsive to national needs.[14]

Within two months of its creation of the HEFCS, the government issued a series of guidelines reaffirming the new relationship. First, the HEFCS were to develop sector-wide methods for allocating resources for teaching and research. Second, they were to articulate what they expected institutions to provide in return for grants and to secure greater fiscal efficiencies as enrolment expanded. Third, they were to increase accountability for research funding received from institutions with designated research specialties. Finally, the HEFCS' assessments of teaching and research quality would determine levels of funding.[15]

By 1993, the HEFCE, with 131 institutions, had directly linked funding to the results and performance of academic units and institutions as determined by research assessment exercises.[16] The new approach transferred a sizeable amount of grant money from distribution on a predictable, formulaic basis and put it in the care of external governmental assessors, who distributed the funds. This system differs radically from the competitive practices in federal research funding in the United States.[17]

Teaching Quality Assessments (TQAS)

Also in 1993, the HEFCE conducted the first TQAS, which emphasized academic performance. However, these procedures did not directly link funding to assessments; such connections were to be phased in gradually.

The Last Decade

During the last decade, the significance and complexity of these comparative assessments of research (RAES) and teaching (TQAS) have increased dramatically. Currently, TQAS use an output rating scheme to measure six dimensions of teaching quality in each institution and then compare the results to those for other institutions.

RAES in 1996 required departments seeking research funds to submit details of their research aims, activities, and achievements. Then the RAE collected statistical and narrative data in eight areas – an overall staff summary, data on active research staff, four examples of publications and other public research–related outputs, research students, research studentships, external research income, research environment, and general observations or other information.[18] Then it presented the information to a panel for each subject area and awarded a grade based on a seven-point scale (1, 2, 3a, 3b, 4, 5, 5*). The final grade was a collective performance evaluation of the department and staff.

After the RAES have concluded, the HEFCS use a funding formula to distribute 90 per cent of all research funding.[19] In 1997 the bulk of funding went to departments based on three figures – the weighted 1996 RAE grade, an average cost for the academic subject, and a volume measure related to the number of active research staffers, students, and assistants. A multiplier effect calculated into the formula disproportionately rewarded higher-graded departments.[20]

Through use of the HEFCS and the performance-based quality- and research-assessment agencies, the government transformed higher education during the last decade. Such annual assessments help shape hiring and retention practices. Institutional rankings and assessments readily translate into annual "League Tables," and parents, students, government officials, and university administrators closely monitor national standings of departments and institutions. HEFCS use these assessments to allocate fiscal resources, based on government criteria. Some of the indicators reflect the growing economic needs of the state by emphasizing technical, industrial, and business demands vis-à-vis higher education. Others reward institutions for enrolling underserved populations and meeting other social needs.

Most recently, the accountability movement has begun experimenting with adjusting salaries of members of faculty and staff. In 2000, a consultation paper from the HEFCE introduced performance-related pay (PRP) as part of a series of measures to address poor teaching and stop the outward migration of top faculty members to other nations.[21] The paper stated that future pay strategies should involve annual performance reviews of all staff, with rewards for individual performance. PRP has already been mooted for university lecturers and researchers. However, the current structure allows universities to forge their own monitoring and assessment arrangements.

Salter and Tapper stated that "the pressures upon the state to control higher education's resources, and force it to respond to what we have called the 'economic dynamic' are overwhelming and inescapable. Modern economies require an ever-changing blend of new knowledge and educational manpower if they are to function effectively and no state can afford to leave its higher education system to its own devices."[22] This is the British government's policy in a nutshell.

PERFORMANCE-BASED REFORMS IN THE UNITED STATES

Higher education in the United States has witnessed a substantial change in its relationship with individual states over the last decade. Because federal involvement is limited primarily to direct student aid, research funding, and certain categoricals, state governments have shaped reform through policies aimed at improving institutional performance. Although the relationship varies from state to state, governments typically provide about 35 per cent of operational funding for public higher education. Legislatures, attempting to get more value from existing resources, increasingly scrutinize how and where these resources are spent. As we see below, their efforts usually involve both performance-based funding and increased accountability.

Performance-Based Funding

In 1978 Tennessee set up a series of performance- or incentive-based funding initiatives focused on measurable outcomes. This approach allowed the state to allocate a percentage of institutional resources based on its own priorities. (The government has a reputation for being long on accountability and short on money.) Today, the system constitutes approximately 5.4 per cent of all resources allocated to public colleges and universities in the state.

Other states adopted performance-related funding policies, in addition to various state and federal mandates that required certain changes. In the early 1990s states began linking some funding for colleges and universities to their achievements in terms of predetermined objectives. By 1996, in approximately seventeen states, appropriation formulas factored in performance.[23] South Carolina is the only state to use performance for allocating nearly all public resources going to colleges and universities.

Accountability

The recent U.S. interest in performance-based funding results from growing public concern for accountability and decreased tax support. As McKeown observes, "[M]any states are either beginning to use or are considering performance funding, which is a natural outgrowth of the current public demand for the most effective use of tax dollars."[24] Although most states have worked to improve higher education, only performance funding directly links financial incentives to achieved results in policy areas that states consider important.

States and governing authorities have adopted other accountability mechanisms that generate comparative institutional data. Authorities' concerns about faculty productivity have led to adjustments in workload policies in more than thirty states.[25] External audiences are increasingly generating and monitoring information related to workload reporting and standards, instructional and research-oriented workloads, and total faculty activities. Governments want comparative institutional data that measure faculty and institutional productivity.

Public campuses in many states are also implementing post-tenure review policies to monitor the effectiveness of tenured members of faculty. In Michigan, Minnesota, Virginia, and Wisconsin, public universities have been pressed to adopt such systems to address growing public concerns about the institution of tenure.

The new pursuit of efficiency has led some state governments to develop policies that decrease the time to complete a degree. Florida, Indiana, and North Carolina are using policies on time to degree and faculty members per degree to force institutions to increase numbers of students while reducing the time needed to complete a degree.

Most states have sought to increase accountability by implementing an measures to determine "value for resources." Ewell and Jones noted four common approaches:

- measurements of "value added" to departing students in the form of inputs, processes, and outcomes
- efficiency measurements to assess use of resources such as faculty, space, and equipment
- measurements of needs and return on investment
- measurements of the effectiveness of higher education in meeting individual needs.[26]

As thirty-eight states anticipate moderate to substantial expansion of enrolment during the next decade, governing authorities and legislatures will remain focused on generating ways to measure the productivity and efficiency of public institutions.[27] The increased U.S. emphasis on accountability, reflected in reports of measurable outcomes and faculty productivity, combined with the growing movement to assess student learning, may continue to push states to attach funding to standards of institutional performance.

SYSTEMIC COMPARISONS

In reviewing performance-based accountability in Britain and the United States, we can see two similarities emerge. First, performance-based funding and budgeting have intensified the tension between policy-makers and higher education because of divergent objectives. Governments prefer indicators that measure institutional efficiency, consumer satisfaction, job placement, and value for resources. They also advocate use of performance measurements as a means of comparing institutional productivity and performance. University administrators and faculty members, in contrast, favour measures that reflect the quality of the educational experience in a manner that elucidates their own specific institutional mission(s). They advocate non-competitive performance measures that help individuals to improve their own performance.

Second, the state's relationship with higher education has evolved from authoritative oversight to active involvement in financial arrangements and economic decisions. Governments intervene directly in order to ensure greater economic efficiency, quality of outcome, student access, and accountability.

Recognizing that these fundamental changes resulted from new economic demands is a critical first step to understanding their popularity. Higher education has evolved into a foundational component of national economic growth. It is being called on to resolve the economic problems of nations, usually without receiving adequate investment. If the primary purpose of higher education is to serve the economy, then the state will hold it accountable in achieving its assigned task.

CONCLUSION

The desire of U.S. state governments and Britain's Parliament for greater control over higher education has been persistent and inescapable. Driven by a new economic dynamic, societies throughout the world are requiring an ever-changing combination of highly skilled workers and knowledge that only education can provide. They expect higher education not only to expand the pool of human capital, but to create new jobs and, through research, to expand the horizons of knowledge. The stakes have become far too great for nations to leave higher education to its own devices. This governmental responsibility has emerged in policy form in the guise of accountability.

Governments have, however, discovered that quality universal higher education requires adequate public funding to maximize economic returns. Governments have responded in different ways, ranging from reasonable funding increases to attempts to squeeze greater efficiencies from already-underfunded systems. Unfortunately, we find Britain largely in the latter situation, along with several U.S. states. In the American case, the challenges associated with expanding access are unlike the enrolment demands of the 1960s. Today, public resources receive closer scrutiny, as policy-makers seek to use higher education to serve more students without substantially increasing per-student financial support. This phenomenon will surely continue to reshape higher education.

NOTES

1 R. Marshall, "The Global Jobs Crisis," in *Foreign Policy: The U.N. in Crisis* (Washington, DC: Carnegie Endowment for International Peace, 1995), 53.

2 "Survey of Universities: The Knowledge Factory," *Economist* (4–10 Oct. 1997), 4.

3 A.B. Cobban, *The Medieval Universities: Their Development and Organization* (London: Methuen and Co., 1975), 76–84.

4 Lord Macaulay, *The History of England*, first pub. 1848–61 (London: Washington Square Press, Inc., 1968), 182.

5 P. Richards, "King and Martyrdom," in *The Cam Review* (Cambridge: Cambridge University Press, 1995), 47.

6 C.J. Lucas, *American Higher Education: A History* (New York: St Martin's Press, 1994), 1.

7 *Report of the Committee of Public Accounts* (London: Department of Education and Science, 1990), ix.

8 See M. Tight, "Do League Tables Contribute to the Development of a Quality Culture? Football and Higher Education Compared," *Higher Education Quarterly* 54, no. 1 (2000): 22–42.

9 See National Center for Public Policy Analysis and Higher Education, *Measuring Up 2000: The State-by-State Report Card for Higher Education* (San Jose, Calif., 2000).

10 P. Partington, "Human Resources Management and Development: A University Policy for Europe," *Journal of the Standing Conference of Rectors, Presidents and Vice Chancellors*, no. 104 (1994), 147.

11 P. Curran, "Competition in UK Higher Education: Competitive Advantage in the Research Assessment Exercise and Porter's Diamond Model," *Higher Education Quarterly* 54, no. 4 (Oct. 2000), 386–91.

12 See B. Salter and T. Tapper, *The State and Higher Education* (Essex, England: Woburn Press, 1994).

13 In 1992 separate funding councils were established for England, Scotland, and Wales.

14 G. Davies, "Higher Education Funding, Performance and Accountability," paper presented at the Oxford Round Table on Educational Policy, Oxford, 1995.

15 Ibid., 6–10.

16 E. El-Khawas and W. Massey, "Britain's 'Performance-Based' System," in W.F. Massey, ed., *Resource Allocation in Higher Education* (Ann Arbor, Mich.: University of Michigan Press, 1995), 223–40.

17 See M. Cave, S. Hanney, M. Henkel, and M. Kogan, *The Use of Performance Indicators in Higher Education: The Challenge of the Quality Movement* (London: Jessica Kingsley, 1997).

18 Curran, "Competition," 390.

19 Ibid., 391.

20 Ibid., 392.

21 See "Rewarding and Developing Staff in Higher Education," paper published by the Higher Education Funding Council for England (2000).

22 Salter and Tapper, *The State*, 18.

23 See J.C. Burke and A.M. Serban, "Performance Funding and Budgeting for Public Higher Education: Current Status and Future Prospects" (Albany, NY: Nelson Rockefeller Institute of Government, State University of New York, 1997), 6; Susan Ruppert, ed., *Charting Higher Education Accountability: A Sourcebook of State-Level Performance Indicators* (Denver, Col.: Education Commission of the States, 1994).

24 Mary P. McKeown, "State Funding Formulas for Public Four-Year Institutions" (Denver, Col.: State Higher Education Executive Officers, Feb. 1996), 6.

25 R. Hauke, "An Update on Faculty Workload Activities among State Higher Education Systems," paper presented at the State Higher Education Fiscal Officers Professional Development Seminar, Aug. 1994, 2.

26 P.T. Ewell and D.P. Jones, "Pointing the Way: Indicators as Policy Tools in Higher Education," in Sandra Rupert, ed., *Charting Higher Education Accountability: A Sourcebook on State-Level Performance Indicators* (Denver, Col.: Education Commission of the States, 1994), 12.

27 *The Chronicle of Higher Education: Almanac Issue* (Aug. 1997), 5–7.

Impediments on the Information Highway: Foreign Jurisdiction over Defamation on the Internet

JAMES J. MINGLE

For academic institutions on both sides of the Atlantic (and the Pacific) the internet is emerging as a favourite medium for students and members of faculty and staff to transmit information, engage in research, stimulate discussion, and exchange messages. This new form of telecommunication, with its universal access, instantaneous use, and global reach, raises important legal issues. U.S. legislatures and courts are attempting to catch up with the internet, as they adapt common law principles, criminal and civil statutes, and constitutional ground rules. Most notably, the U.S. Congress has enacted statutes that accommodate free expression, insulate internet service providers (ISPs) from defamation liability for third-party communication, attempt to curb pornography, and prescribe manageable rules governing copyright infringement.[1]

The internet's lack of geographical boundaries exposes U.S. academic institutions to the jurisdiction of foreign courts for legally offensive communications transmitted over their network servers and retrieved (and read) on the computer of an individual in another country.

The liability risk to the entities providing internet access will vary significantly, depending on how the foreign country's legal system treats the interplay among jurisdictional rules, principles of free expression, standards of defamation, and internet use. When an ISP is pulled into a foreign court, will the court harmonize these critical concepts in the interest of accommodating the internet as a vital medium of information and commerce? Or will it decline to reconcile the tension and allow claims of personal defamation to trump the free speech inherent in internet use? Will it treat the ISP as a "conduit" of messages, akin to a telephone company, and thus shield the ISP from defamation liability? Or will it cast a defendant university providing network access as a "publisher," presumed able to "control" the content of the transmitted information, and thus subject it to heightened liability?

The economic and policy stakes are high, both for providers of access and for users of the internet. Contending with defamation risks in pro-plaintiff jurisdictions could force ISPs to set up content-screening systems to monitor potentially libellous communications or perhaps explore ways to implant barriers in their computer servers that would technologically restrict access to and transmission of e-mail messages and electronic postings by residents of legally hostile countries. Either approach would be financially and technologically daunting – and encumber free speech.

This risk is not abstract. A resident of England recently sued two U.S. universities – Cornell and Minnesota – in London courts for statements that students communicated via the internet that that person claimed were defamatory. These universities were forced to choose between two equally undesirable alternatives: to engage foreign counsel to defend the suits on grounds of compelling principle to seek cash settlements. Two dramatically different standards of defamation liability came into play.

I first explore *Godfrey v. Cornell*, which reveals a disturbing aspect of internet use resulting from its global reach. I then look at U.S. law regarding libel on the internet and next examine the much more restrictibe British law on libel and its effect on the decision in *Godfrey v. Demon Internet*. I finally propose measures – internet, judicial, legislative, and international – that may reduce the liability risk of universities on both sides of the Atlantic, which (like Cornell) typically facilitate millions of electronic communications per day – or that may at least render the risk more predictable. An international treaty might provide for adjudication of internet defamation claims by deferring to the jurisdictional and substantive law of the country of origin of the offending communication.

A CASE STUDY: A FOREIGN LIBEL SUIT
AGAINST CORNELL

In October 1997, a British resident sued Cornell University in the High Court of Justice in London. The plaintiff, Laurence Godfrey, sought substantial damages for statements that a Cornell graduate student named Michael Dolenga allegedly posted on an internet newsgroup in December 1994 and April 1995.[2] In his complaint,[3] Godfrey alleged: "Cornell falsely and maliciously *published ... defamatory* words ... *read in England and Wales* ... on the [internet] UseNet Newsgroup known as 'soc.culture.canada' ..." (emphasis added).

Godfrey, a British scientist, did not allege that the student functioned as Cornell's "agent" or that the university was vicariously responsible. Rather, he transformed Cornell's role as an ISP into that of a publisher, rendering it responsible for the content of the student's postings. The plaintiff also alleged that Cornell's failure to withdraw Dolenga's privileges of computer access after Godfrey had notified it of the initial defamatory postings made it strictly liable under English law as a publisher of the student's subsequent statements.

This lawsuit was the first of its kind for Cornell. As a large, complex research institution, Cornell is accustomed to defending an assortment of contract, tort, and civil rights actions in various venues. But it had never defended a lawsuit in a foreign jurisdiction for statements over the internet made by a student residing in the United States.[4]

Settling meritless cases for cash is a concept foreign to Cornell, so it quickly discarded this option. Although the university's assets in England are minimal,[5] it resolved to mount a vigorous defence based on the same strategic considerations animating a response to any contested action against Cornell: either force the plaintiff to drop his case or vindicate the vital policy principles in court.[6]

Cornell forged a compelling defence to Godfrey's defamation claims in its responsive pleadings (the "Statement of Defence"), in anticipation of filing a comprehensive motion to dismiss (characterized as a "Motion to Strike"). Cornell advanced three principal arguments. First, Cornell's role as an ISP is no different from that of a telephone company or a mail carrier, neither of which bears legal responsibility for the content of third-party communications. Second, it cannot monitor the staggering volume and velocity of personal e-mail messages and postings that individuals launch into cyberspace via the university's server.[7] Third, it would be completely contrary to paramount American principles of free speech, personal privacy, and due process for Cornell to censor or control the content of electronically transmitted statements.[8]

How would this defence fare on its merits? If Godfrey had pursued his defamation action in New York, instead of in London, Cornell would have swiftly prevailed on a motion to dismiss. However, in the first case in England involving an attempt to hold an American ISP liable as a publisher,[9] Cornell's chances were unpredictable. They depended directly on whether the court adopted an expansive view of the common law "innocent dissemination" defence and imported American rights of free speech into the analysis.[10]

The same case could produce opposite conclusions in two countries that share the same language and similar cultures – and common law. To understand such a study in contrasts requires a brief exposition of how defamation law has evolved in the United States and England.

INTERNET DEFAMATION IN THE UNITED STATES

Factoring in the First Amendment

Common law principles of defamation in the United States and England were parallel until the 1960s. Since then, however, several dynamic developments in American law have distanced it from English libel law. A trilogy of cases in the U.S. Supreme Court between 1964 and 1974 focused on freedom of expression, elevating and shifting the standard and burden of proof in defamation cases that implicate the first amendment to the U.S. constitution.

In its watershed decision, *New York Times v. Sullivan*, 376 U.S. 254, 279, 84 S.Ct. 710, 726 (1964), the Supreme Court concluded that the first amendment "prohibits a public official from recovering damages for a defamatory falsehood." A "public official" plaintiff must prove that the purportedly defamatory statement "was made with 'actual malice' – that is, with knowledge that it was false or with reckless disregard of whether it was false or not" (279–80). A few years later, in *Curtis Publishing Company v. Butts*, 388 U.S. 130, 155, 87 S.Ct. 1975, 1991 (1967), the court extended the same heightened standard of proof to "public figures" who sue for defamation.

The Supreme Court also altered common law principles when a private-person plaintiff assails as defamatory an article rooted in a "matter of public concern." In *Gertz v. Robert Welch, Inc.*, 418 U.S. 323, 94 S.Ct. 2997 (1974), the court emphasized that a private person cannot simply allege defamation and invoke strict liability principles against the publisher (340). Instead, such a plaintiff must show fault or negligence on the part of the publisher.[11]

Congressional Accommodation of ISPs

In the *Sullivan*, *Butts*, and *Gertz* cases between 1964 and 1974, the U.S. Supreme Court protected conventional media with the first amendment in order to promote public criticism, commentary, and discourse. The emergence of the internet as a medium of universal communication prompted Congress to consider shielding ISPs from defamation liability.[12] Legislators debated whether to accord entities providing access to the internet a qualified privilege as publishers or distributors of third-party electronic communicators or to give them blanket immunity. In the Communications Decency Act of 1996, Congress resolved to immunize "interactive computer services,"[13] removing them from the risky role of publishers or distributors. Section 230(c)(1) stipulates: "No provider or user of an interactive computer service shall be treated as the publisher or speaker of any information provided by another information content provider."

Subsequent court decisions fortified this statutory immunity. In *Zeran v. America Online, Inc.*, 129 F.3d 327, 331 (4th Cir. 1997), the federal appeals court spotlighted critical policy issues: given the "staggering" volume and velocity of information transmitted, it would be "impossible for service providers to screen each of their millions of postings for possible problems." So, if the courts imposed publisher-style liability, ISPs would choose "to severely restrict the number and type of messages posted" (331). This in turn would have an "obvious chilling effect on speech" (331). Consequently, the court noted, "Congress considered the weight of speech interests implicated and chose to immunize service providers to avoid such a restrictive effect" (331).

The Fourth Circuit resolved another critical question raised by the plaintiff in *Zeran*. It construed section 230 of the Communications Decency Act as evincing congress's intention to immunize ISPs even when they are "notified" of potentially defamatory postings and fail to remove them (333).

Recent case law in other jurisdictions is fully in accord with the Fourth Circuit's decision in *Zeran*. Precedents in *Blumenthal v. Drudge and America Online, Inc.*, 992 F. Supp. 44 (D.C. 1998), the precedents reject a defamation claim against an ISP for posting an electronic publication licensed from a third party, even though the editorial rights were reserved and the relationship with the author was actively publicized. Relying heavily on *Zeran*, the court stated:

[Under the Communications Decency Act, Congress] made the legislative judgment to effectively immunize providers of interactive computer services from civil liability in tort with respect to material disseminated by them but created by others ... Congress decided not to treat providers of interactive computer services like other information providers such as newspaper magazines or television and radio stations, all of which may be held liable for publishing or distributing obscene or defamatory material written or prepared by others.[14]

Similarly, in *Ben Ezra, Weinstein, and Co. v. America Online, Inc.*, 206 F.3d 980, 986 (10th Cir. 2000), the federal appellate court broadly construed section 230, noting that it bars imposing publisher-type liability on a service provider for exercising editorial and self-regulatory functions. In another recent case, the highest state court in New York affirmed summary judgment in favour of an ISP (AISP@) where a user had posted vulgar messages on the ISP's electronic bulletin boards and transmitted libellous e-mail via its server. *See Lunney v. Prodigy Services Co.*, 733 NE 2d 539, 540 (NY 1999). Applying established tort principles, the court declared that the ISP was entitled to the qualified privilege accorded telephone and telegraphy companies: "Prodigy's role in transmitting e-mail is akin to that of a telephone company, which neither wants nor expects to superintend the content of its subscribers' conversations. In this respect an ISP, like a telephone company, is merely a conduit" (542).

ENGLISH DEFAMATION LAW: A DISREGARD OF FREE SPEECH

Principles and Internet Concerns

In stark contrast to the pivotal U.S. legal developments, English defamation law has remained basically "unchanged from the earlier common law period" (*Telnikoff*, 702 A.2d at 247). It has traditionally tilted heavily towards protecting personal reputations and has shown little regard for free expression. As Smolla has observed, "British law recognizes no special protection for defamation actions arising from critiques of public figures or public officials, routinely imposing large damage awards in cases involving what American courts would characterize as core political discourse."[15] As the Maryland Court of Appeals noted in *Telnikoff*, the "significant ... differences are rooted in historic and fundamental public policy differences concerning freedom of the press and speech" (248).

In U.S. courts, plaintiffs who assail articles that address matters of public concern must establish fault on the part of the defendant publisher, proving either "deliberate disregard of the truth" (public officials or public figures) or "negligence" (private plaintiffs). In England, however, fault is not an element of proof.[16] Indeed, a publisher may be liable even if the defendant held the honest belief that the defamatory statement was true and published the statement without negligence. Furthermore, English law presumes defamatory statements false unless a defendant proves them true.[17] U.S. courts consider the "context" in which the statements appeared, examining broadly whether the publication addressed "matters of public concern." In England, in contrast, "[c]ontext appears to be eliminated from a court's determination of whether a statement is considered fact or comment."[18]

English defamation law accords absolutely no accommodation to the internet. In fact, legal developments in the United States and England have moved in dramatically different directions. In 1996, the U.S. Congress enacted the Communications Decency Act, which immunizes ISPs from tort liability for statements posted or transmitted by third parties. In the same year, the British Parliament adopted the Defamation Act, which not only makes no reference to the internet, but arguably narrows the common law defence available to publishers.[19] As a recent article noted, "the general principles of libel remain the same whatever the medium, whether it is newspapers, or the Internet ... The Defamation Act 1996 makes clear that liability can be attached to any party that has a hand in the publication of a defamatory statement and they can be held joint and severally liable."[20]

Godfrey v. Demon Internet

In 1999, a High Court in London reached the opposite conclusion to that of the *Zeran* court on virtually identical facts.[21] In *Godfrey v.*

Demon Internet Ltd., 4 All ER 342 (QB 1999), the English court considered, on a pre-trial motion, a defamation action maintained by Laurence Godfrey against Demon Internet, a British counterpart to America Online. Godfrey, a familiar litigant against ISPs (including Cornell University),[22] sought to hold Demon Internet legally responsible as a "publisher" of allegedly defamatory statements that a third party had posted on the soc.culture.thai newsgroup. Godfrey claimed that the postings were "squalid, obscene and defamatory" and demanded that Demon Internet (345). When the company failed to remove the article, Godfrey sued.[23]

The court rejected Demon's contention that it was an "innocent" carrier of the offensive postings and allowed the case to proceed to trial (352). Acknowledging that this was the first judicial decision in England and Wales involving defamation on the internet, the court examined the legislative history of the "innocent dissemination" defence under the Defamation Act of 1996.[24] The court emphasized that the defence "is available only if, having taken all reasonable care, the defendant had no reason to suspect that his [publication contributed to the defamation of the plaintiff]."[25] The court also chronicled cases dating back to 1937, noting that "[a]t Common Law liability for the publication of defamatory material was strict" (347). The court relied on the "Golf Club notice board case," *Bryne v. Deane*, in which a plaintiff sought to hold the owner of a golf club strictly liable as a publisher when it failed to remove offensive graffiti from a club wall: "The test … is this: having regard to all the facts of the case[,] is the proper inference that by not removing the defamatory matter the defendant really made himself responsible for its continued presence in the place where it had been put?" (348, quoting *Bryne v. Deane*, 1 KB 818, 837 [1937]).

The court also discussed several recent American cases that dealt with defamation actions involving ISPs but dismissed them as offering "only marginal assistance because of the different approach to defamation across the Atlantic" (348). The court disregarded *Zeran* because U.S. statute immunized ISPs, while Britain's Defamation Act "did not adopt this approach or have this purpose" (351). The court did not even address, let alone acknowledge, the important policy interests and practical problems that would flow from a finding that ISPs are liable as publishers for third-party statements posted on their metaphysical "wall."[26] Justice Morland concluded that Demon *published* the defamatory posting; after receiving Godfrey's notice, it "knew of the defamatory content of the posting" and so "cannot avail themselves [*sic*] of the defense of innocent dissemination" (352).

Ramifications of the Demon Internet Decision

The High Court's decision in *Demon Internet* in April 1999 confirmed the worst fears of ISPs. As one English barrister observed: "The ramifications of this decision are that the defence of innocent dissemination will not be available to those ISPs that store material in addition to those who exercise any form of editorial control over their newsgroups."[27] Most ISPs, including both commercial services and nonprofit universities, obviously fall within this ambit of increased risk.

The decision did not directly affect Cornell University, because Godfrey had dropped his case against Cornell the previous year. Cognizant of Cornell's resolve to litigate the case through trial and appeal (if necessary) in the English courts, Godfrey discontinued his case against Cornell in September 1998, under terms, *inter alia*, that "neither party paid the other any money."[28] In early 1999, while its motion to dismiss on jurisdictional grounds was pending – and also prior to the decision in *Demon Internet* – Godfrey settled his internet defamation case against the University of Minnesota on similar terms.

If Godfrey's 1997 lawsuit against Cornell had unnerved American ISPs,[29] Demon Internet's decision to settle its defamation dispute with Godfrey in 2000 disturbed all those who value the free flow of electronic information. Sarah Lyall reported: "A British Internet service provider has agreed to pay a substantial sum to a physicist who says he was libeled in messages posted on electronic bulletin boards carried by the company, in a move that lawyers fear will severely curtail people's ability to speak freely in cyberspace. The company, Demon Internet, said on [30 March 2000] that it would pay about $25,000 in damages ... as well as Mr. Godfrey's court costs, which are likely to come to several hundred thousand dollars."[30]

The court's pre-trial decision in April 1999 rejecting Demon Internet's "innocent" carrier defence undoubtedly troubled the company as it approached trial. But why did Demon Internet not seek a reversal by litigating the case through the trial and appellate levels in the English courts, as its U.S. counterparts had done in several cases involving internet defamation claims?[31] In any event, U.S. universities (and other ISPs) now face a worst-case scenario: a constant risk of defamation suits in English courts for third-party e-mail and postings that they cannot possibly control, subject to relaxed jurisdiction rules and strict liability substantive standards. This is an intolerable legal predicament that calls for thoughtful legislative remedies.

CRITICAL NEED TO CRAFT REMEDIES

Academic institutions – in tandem with commercial on-line companies – can consider remedies to reduce the risk of internet defamation suits in forums foreign to more familiar and favourable U.S. legal standards. These remedies, outlined below, range from self-imposed practical controls to an international treaty.

Self-Imposed Measures

An Internal Complaint Response System   The most cautious approach for ISPs would be to establish an internal system of "complaint response" to review and respond to "notifications" received from British residents that a particular posting is defamatory. The decision in *Demon Internet* effectively requires ISPs to adopt this approach in order to avoid potential strict liability as publishers. Even though such a system is necessary only for British complainants, ISPs would still have to establish and administer such a system, and it would have "a chilling effect on the freedom of Internet speech."[32] As the court pointed out in *Zeran*: "Because service providers would be subject to liability only for the publication of information, and not for its removal, they would have a natural incentive simply to remove messages upon notification, whether the contents were defamatory or not" (129 F.3d at 333).

Geographical Screening Devices   Conceivably, ISPs could band together to explore ways of implanting devices in their computer servers that would deny English residents access to newsgroups on U.S. ISPs' computer systems. Such barriers are currently available to limit password access to an ISP's websites. However, engineering an effective barrier would require a technological treaty of sorts among American and English ISPs. And even then, English internet users could log onto newsgroup postings via ISP servers in other countries. Just the threat, however, that U.S. ISPs are considering such technical barriers would deliver a potent political message. It could cause an uproar among English internet users, who in turn may press their leaders to amend the country's defamation laws.

The Judicial Route

Shifting from these conservative (and technologically challenging) approaches, a bolder option for ISPs would be to continue to do business as usual: eschew any editorial responsibility to review and remove potentially defamatory postings and brace for a *Godfrey*-like defamation suit in England. And, like Cornell University (but unlike Demon Internet), the ISP would have to resolve to contest the defamation case as far as the highest court in England or to force the plaintiff to fold his or her cards along the way. This option is obviously risky and costly, but it could lead to new case law recognizing a proper balance among defamation claims, free expression, and internet use.[33]

For defamation claims arising after October 2000, an ISP sued in England may improve its prospects by invoking Britain's Human Rights Act (HRA) of 1998.[34] This statute, intended "to give further effect to rights and freedoms guaranteed under the European Convention on Human Rights," codifies a series of basic human rights, including "freedom of expression."[35] English law had previously acknowledged an *implied* right of free expression, although the courts gave superseding effect to countervailing common law and statutes (as illustrated by the court's interpretation of the Defamation Act in *Demon Internet*).[36] Under article 10 of the HRA, however, "[e]veryone has the right to freedom of expression. This right shall include freedom to hold opinions and to receive and impart information and ideas without interference by public authority and regardless of frontiers."[37]

Now that English law *expressly* recognizes principles of free expression, ISPs appear to have a fortified argument to mitigate defamation liability on the internet. The critical test remains, however, whether English courts will give pre-emptive weight to article 10 of the HRA, or will adhere to a broad interpretation of rights to reputation protected by the Defamation Act. The HRA itself sends conflicting signals: section 12(4) enjoins courts to give "particular regard to the importance of the Convention right to freedom of expression," while section 10(2) qualifies section 10(1)'s clause on "Freedom of Expression":

The exercise of these freedoms, since it carries with it duties and responsibilities, *may be subject to such formalities, conditions, restrictions or penalties as are prescribed by law* and are necessary in a democratic society, in the interests of national security, territorial integrity or public safety, for the prevention of disorder or crime, for the protection of health or morals, *for the protection of the reputation or rights of others,* for preventing the disclosure of information received in confidence, or *for maintaining the authority and impartiality of the judiciary.*[38]

Legislative Routes

The legislative approach clearly has the most enduring effect for ISPS but may also be the most difficult to accomplish. It requires a lobbying campaign and engaged legislators to amend statutes either in Britain or the United States.

Amending the British Legislation   One option is to amend Britain's Defamation Act of 1996 to make its "publisher responsibility" provisions like those in the U.S. Communications Decency Act of 1996. An amendment that would be most protective of ISPs on both sides of the Atlantic would explicitly incorporate immunity for ISPS for third-party messages that they transmit or post on their services (excluding, like the U.S. act, information that ISPS create).

However, given Parliament's usual slowness in modifying common law, it would probably be more realistic to press for an amendment to the Defamation Act of 1996 that provides a qualified privilege for ISPS. For example, Parliament could amend the "innocent dissemination" defence[39] as follows:

(5) In determining for the purposes of this section [pertaining to the innocent dissemination defense] whether a person took reasonable care, or had reason to believe that what he did caused or contributed to the publication of a defamatory statement, regard shall be had to –
(a) the extent of his responsibility for the content of the statement or the decision to publish it,
(b) the nature or circumstances of the publication, including the type of medium in which the statement appeared and the degree of difficulty for the publisher to control or monitor the content of information created or communicated by third parties, and
(c) the previous conduct or character of the author, editor or publisher.[40]

Amending the U.S. Legislation   A second option is to amend the U.S. Communications Decency Act of 1996 to insulate ISPS from liability for intentional defamation. To extend this immunity beyond U.S.

borders, Congress could insert a new provision into section 230 to create a cause of action for ISPs to obtain indemnification from any party that has sued and secured monetary damages against the ISP in a foreign jurisdiction, in instances where such foreign judgment is predicated on a tort theory that "is inconsistent with this section."[41]

As an alternative – and more intermediate – approach, Congress could adapt a new provision from the Maryland Uniform Foreign-Money Judgments Recognition Act, which the Maryland Court of Appeals invoked to bar enforcement of English libel decisions:[42] "A foreign judgment need not be recognized by any federal district court if the cause of action on which the judgment is based is repugnant to the public policy of the United States, as reflected in this section."

An International Treaty?

The final approach – daunting to achieve, yet most broadly protective of American ISPs – would be an international treaty encompassing all countries linked to the internet. There are several bilateral and transnational treaties that could serve as templates. The Berne Convention, 1971, which protects copyright, stipulates different "choice of law" ground rules depending on the type of dispute.[43] For the duration of copyright protection, for example, the Berne Convention provides that the law of the copyrighted work's country of origin shall prevail.[44] Thus the country asked to entertain the suit for copyright infringement looks to the law applicable where the work appeared.[45]

An internet treaty could draw on the familiar "law of the flag" principle of international maritime law, which decides what jurisdiction controls the law for tort occurrences on the seas.[46] Thus the laws of the country where the electronic communication originated would govern adjudication of defamation claims against ISPs for third-party communications.

CONCLUSION

If the internet is as an information highway, it has no boundaries, because it interconnects countless countries. Academe has helped design and construct this system and facilitates access to and use of it. But as ISPs, academic institutions cannot police or control the conduct, direction, or speed of travellers. Nor can ISPs keep the internet free of impediments or minimize roadblocks – only makers of public policy can do so. U.S. authorities (Congress and the courts) have done so by reducing the legal risk to ISPs and by advancing the free flow of information. Other countries have not. I have mapped out ways to accomplish these critical objectives. It is incumbent on the public authorities in Britain and elsewhere to remove obstacles to the international information highway, if the internet is to reach its enormous potential as an inexpensive, swift, ubiquitous, and useful information and commercial medium.

NOTES

1 See, for example, Communications Decency Act (CDA) of 1996, 47 USC 230 (1996); Digital Millennium Copyright Act, 17 USC 512 (1998).

2 Also in October 1997 (on the same day: 29 October), Godfrey filed suit in the same English court against the University of Minnesota and a former engineering student for purportedly defamatory postings on the internet newsgroup "soc.culture.thai." Godfrey's claims against Minnesota were virtually identical to those lodged against Cornell.

3 Godfrey also sued the graduate student, Michael Dolenga.

4 Godfrey, however, is no stranger to this type of litigation. In 1994, he sued a fellow physicist, Philip Hallan-Baker, for libel stemming from internet postings challenging Godfrey's professional competence. Besides suing Cornell and Minnesota, Godfrey maintained defamation actions in English courts against several other foreign entities – reportedly including several Canadian universities, the *Toronto Star*, Melbourne PC Users Group, and New Zealand Telecom – claiming that they were "publishers" of defamatory postings and statements. See Matt Hines, *Newsbytes News Network Release* (26 March 1999) <http://www.newsbytes.com>.

More recently, in a case discussed in the second part of this article, Godfrey sued Demon Internet, a popular internet on-line service in Britain, for defamation in connection with a third-party article on soc.culture.thai, a newsgroup carried by Demon's server. See *Godfrey v. Demon Internet Ltd.*, 4 All ER 342 (QB 1999); Carl S. Kaplan, "English Court May Test U.S. Ideals on Online Speech," *Cyber Law Journal* 33 (5 June 1998), <http://www.nytimes.com/>.

All these suits reportedly resulted in monetary settlements for undisclosed sums.

5 Another (admittedly venturesome) option would be to decline to
   contest the claims in England, take a default judgment, and fight any
   attempt by Godfrey to enforce his libel judgment in a U.S. court. Here,
   Cornell could draw on a Maryland decision in 1997, *Telnikoff v.*
   Matusevitch, 702 A.2d 230 (Md. 1997), where the state appellate court
   refused to enforce a libel judgment in London on the grounds that
   English libel laws are repugnant to constitutional principles of free
   speech embedded in Maryland law.

6 Because British jurisdictional rules are relatively pliable, our solicitors
   and barristers in London discouraged a threshold challenge on jurisdictional grounds. They believed it likely that the court would focus on
   the fact that the student's internet postings "originated" on the Cornell
   computer server (even though the transmissions would travel over
   numerous other servers before arriving in England) and would "infer"
   that individuals in England read the postings. The University of
   Minnesota chose this tactic and filed a comprehensive motion to
   dismiss the case for lack of jurisdiction.

7 Cornell also pointed out that postings on its server remain only for
   seven days and can be accessed only by persons granted Cornell's net
   IDs (i.e., passwords). Cornell has no control whatsoever over electronic
   messages and postings transmitted instantaneously over the myriad
   servers that make up the internet.

8 Cornell also charted, in its statement of defence, documentary evidence
   asserting that the plaintiff had engaged in a purposeful pattern of pro-
   voking offensive exchanges by hurling ethnic insults at Canadian and
   Thai citizens via the "soc.culture.canada" and "soc.culture.thai" Usenet
   newsgroups. The English court's pre-trial ruling in *Demon Internet* (discussed below) addressed a comparable defence and stated that "on the
   basis of [this] ... [d]efence any award of damages to [Godfrey] is likely
   to be very small." *Demon Internet*, 4 All ER at 352.

9 Although Godfrey launched his similar suit against the University of
   Minnesota at the same time (October 1997), that action chose to contest
   jurisdiction. Thus Cornell's positioning of its defence for an
   adjudication on the merits moved its case ahead of Minnesota's.

10 According to our English solicitors and barristers, if the courts
   interpreted the "innocent dissemination" defence, anchored in the
   Defamation Act of 1996, as essentially codifying common law
   principles governing publishers' liability, Cornell's prospects were
   favourable. Conversely, a restrictive reading could increase its risk.

11 See *Demon Internet*, 4 All ER at 347. In *Philadelphia Newspapers, Inc.*
   v. Hepps, 475 U.S. 767, 768, 106 S.Ct. 1558, 1559 (1986), the U.S.
   Supreme Court extended the essential-proof elements set forth in *Gertz*
   and shifted to the plaintiff the burden of showing falsity of the
   defamatory statement, as well as fault on the part of the defendant,
   "where a newspaper publishes speech of pubic concern."

12 See Communications Decency Act (CDA) of 1996 at 230(a).

13 Section 230 defines "interactive computer service" as "any information
   service, system, or access software provider that provides or enables
   computer access by multiple users to a computer server, including
   specifically a service or system that provides access to the Internet and
   such systems operated or services offered by libraries or *educational*
   institutions" (emphasis added). CDA at 230(f)(2).

14 *Blumenthal*, 992 F.Supp. at 49.

15 Ibid. at 248, quoting Rodney A. Smolla, "Law of Defamation" 1.03(3)
   (St Paul: West Group, 1986).

16 See *Demon Internet*, 4 All ER at 347.

17 See *Telnikoff*, 702 A.2d at 236 n. 10. In addition, a defendant risks
   punitive damages if he or she pleads truth but fails to prove it. See
   ibid. at 247.

18 Ibid. at 248. "English defamation law presumes that a statement is one
   of fact, and the burden is on the defendant to prove 'fair comment.'"

19 See Defamation Act 1996, c. 31, 1. See also generally: S. Ghandi and
   J. James, "The English Law of Blasphemy and the European Conven-
   tion on Human Rights," *European Convention on Human Rights Law*
   Review, 430 (1998).

20 Adam Cannon, "Internet Libel: Who Is Responsible?," *New Law Journal*
   150 (2000), 6920, 90.

21 The court in *Zeran* interpreted section 230 as preventing courts from
   entertaining defamation claims that would place ISPs in a publisher's
   or distributor's role, even where the ISP had knowledge of the
   defamatory content of messages posted on electronic bulletin boards.

22 See text at note 4 above.

23 See Sarah Lyall, "British Internet Provider to Pay Physicist Who Says
   e-Bulletin Board Libeled Him," *New York Times*, 1 April 2000, A5
   (describing this litigation and Demon Internet's subsequent decision to
   settle the case).

24 See *Demon Internet*, 4 All ER at 343, 346–7. The act defines the "innocent dissemination" defence as follows: "In defamation proceedings a
   person has a defence if he shows that – (a) he was not the author,

editor or publisher of the statement complained of, (b) he took reasonable care in relation to its publication, *and* (c) he did not know, and had no reason to believe, that what he did caused or contributed to the publication of a defamatory statement." Defamation Act 1996, c. 31, 1(1).

25 *Demon Internet*, 4 All ER at 346 (quoting Lord Mackay, LC, during debate on the Defamation Bill).

26 The court also discussed several other U.S. cases including *Lunney*, finding that the defendant ISP in that case would clearly have been the publisher under English law. Ibid., at 351–2.

27 Cannon, "Internet Libel," 92.

28 The publicly released settlement terms state:

> Dr. Laurence Godfrey's lawsuit against Cornell University has been withdrawn on agreed terms under which neither party pays the other any money.
> Dr. Godfrey, a British citizen, commenced proceedings in the English High Court on Oct. 29, 1997 against Cornell University and Michael Dolenga, a Canadian citizen and former Cornell University biochemistry graduate student. Dr. Godfrey sought damages against both defendants for the publication in England and Wales via the Internet of statements made by Mr. Dolenga between December 1994 and April 1995. Cornell University believes that Mr. Dolenga's use of the Internet as alleged in Dr. Godfrey's lawsuit was offensive and irresponsible. Furthermore, Cornell University has found no basis to support Mr. Dolenga's statements complained of by Dr. Godfrey. In the circumstances, Cornell University is prepared to co-operate with Dr. Godfrey in his proceedings against Mr. Dolenga. Dr. Godfrey has obtained a default judgment against Mr. Dolenga as a result of Mr. Dolenga's failure to defend these proceedings. Now that the proceedings against Cornell University have been settled, damages will be assessed against Mr. Dolenga and Dr. Godfrey anticipates obtaining a substantial award by the Court.

29 Consider the following commentary in Kaplan, "English Court May Test U.S. Ideals," concerning Godfrey's lawsuit against Cornell:

> In what many lawyers believe is the first case of its kind, and one that could test whether expansive American notions of free expression can prevail on the global Internet, an American University is being sued for libel in England for its role in the online posting of a student's statements about an English citizen ... Many Internet lawyers have been predicting that Internet service providers and private individuals would eventually be sued in libel-friendly foreign courts – raising havoc with American notions of free expression ... Barry Steinhardt,

president of the Electronic Frontier Foundation, a civil liberties group, added that the Godfrey case was an impossible situation, preposterous. To the extent that ISPs are subject to idiosyncratic [foreign] laws of defamation, it is more likely they will censor their users. (1, 4, 6–7)

30 Lyall, "British Internet Provider," A5.
31 See, for example, *Zeran*, 129 F.3d 327; *Lunney*, 723 N.E.2d 539; *Ben, Ezra, Weinstein*, 206 F.3d 980. See also *Doe v. America Online*, 718 So. 2d 385 (Fla. Dist. Ct. App., 4th Dist. 1998).
32 *Zeran*, 129 F.3d at 333. Cornell has an internal system that refers any complaints about "irresponsible computer use" by students to the university's Campus Code of Conduct. Proof of violations within this due-process framework could lead to disciplinary sanctions ranging from restraints on computer access to expulsion from the university. Cornell advised Godfrey of this system after he notified it of the first (of four) offensive postings by Dolenga. But he refused to avail himself of this process and filed his defamation suit anyway.
33 Even if the outcome were unfavourable (and if we assume minimal assets in England), the defendant ISP could resist a U.S. action to enforce the judgment. See note 5 above.
34 See United Kingdom, Human Rights Act 1998, c. 42, sched. 1.
35 Ibid. at sched. 1, art. 10.
36 In contrast, the U.S. first amendment, like other constitutional clauses, pre-empts state and federal statutes, regulations, and common law that U.S. courts determine conflict with constitutional provisions.
37 Human Rights Act 1998, c. 42, sched. 1, art. 10(1).
38 Ibid. at art. 10(2) (emphasis added).
39 See note 24 above.
40 Defamation Act 1996, c. 31, 1(5).
41 As in other legislatively or judicially created causes of action, of course, the U.S. plaintiff must establish jurisdiction over the English defendant.
42 See *Telnikoff*, 702 A.2d at 238 n. 12 (quoting Maryland's Uniform Foreign-Money Judgments Recognition Act).
43 See Sam Ricketson, *The Berne Convention for the Protection of Literary and Artistic Works: 1886–1986* (London: Sweet & Maxwell Ltd, May 1989), 5.52, 5.53 (1987).
44 See ibid., 7.1–7.16.
45 Two other choices of law provisions apply under the Berne Convention in other circumstances. Under one, "national treatment," the nation where the litigant seeks judicial protection and remedies applies

its own copyright laws both to its citizens and to foreign nationals. Under the other, the country may protect the foreign work in accordance with the specific rules or standards contained in the international treaty itself. Ibid., 1.27, 1.34, 1.35, 4.2, 5.52.

46 See Note, "Conflicts on the Net: Choice of Law in Transnational Cyberspace," *Vand. J. Transnat'l* 29 (1996), 75, discussing complexities surrounding "conflicts of laws" and "choice of law" arising from transactional tort and contract claims.

Rising Costs and the Survival of America's Small Private Colleges

JOHN H. MOORE

In the last few years, attention has focused on the cost of higher education in the United States. Sparked by rapidly rising tuition fees, especially at private colleges, public concern culminated in Congress's establishment in 1997 of the National Commission on the Cost of Higher Education, which reported to Congress in January 1998.[1] Apart from generating the occasional headline,[2] the matter has rested there ever since. Certainly, increases in tuition fees have moderated, but public attention evaporates quickly.

The commission's report emphasized the crucial difference between price and cost. Parents and students are concerned about the price of college – fees for tuition and for other services that they must pay. And they worry about the net price – what they actually pay after they have obtained the best deal possible from the institution.

College administrators look carefully at price, of course, since that is one of the margins along which they compete for students. But for them cost is a different matter. The cost is what they must pay to provide educational services. For virtually every institution, it is greater than price; Winston et al. estimate that on average tuition fees paid by students cover about one-third of total educational costs.[3] For private institutions, the fraction is about 45 per cent; for public ones, only 10 per cent. Colleges must cover total costs, at least for long-run survival; they must make up the difference between costs and fees from other sources – endowment earnings, gifts, grants, and other kinds of what Winston calls "donative" resources, which we call "fund raising."

Survival requires competing successfully for revenues from students and for other donative resources. We in small private colleges face competition from many sources, and the competition increases constantly. First, we compete with each other, and we are all working hard to obtain students and funds. This competition itself creates upward pressure on costs, as we see below. We also compete increasingly with public universities and other institutions.

In Pennsylvania, where my college is located, the Pennsylvania State University creates strong competition for all the private colleges. And competition from Penn State is growing as the university extends its four-year programs to its branch campuses around the state. We are also beginning to feel the effects of competition from the private, for-profit sector, which I take to include not only well-known institutions such as the University of Phoenix, but also college-equivalent courses that corporations offer to their employees. Finally, there is the internet, through which colleges and universities can extend their reach far beyond their immediate physical sites. The market – and the competition that it affords – thus reach far beyond their previous limits.

This situation is familiar – constant pressure on costs, growing competition, the search for funds to cover costs, and the need to find ways to survive. And some small colleges do not make it. The cover story on the 12 May 2000 issue of the *Chronicle of Higher Education* deals with the closing of Bradford College and the shaky status of Trinity College in Vermont. The article also lists five other private four-year colleges that have closed in the last few years.[4] So the threat is real.

My background lay in economics, which is concerned typically with the for-profit sector. However, economists have done much work on non-profits, whose operating characteristics are very different and very interesting. I discuss the economics of independent small colleges – first, factors driving costs upward and, second, subsidies, cost control, and "value for money" – and the implications for survival.

"COST DRIVERS"

Ten years ago, Malcolm Getz and John J. Siegfried published a detailed study of costs in higher education and their changes between 1978–

79 and 1988–89.[5] They provide insight into the structure of costs in colleges and universities.

The study grew out of concern about the rising costs of higher education, and the authors considered a number of explanatory hypotheses. Perhaps their most striking conclusion was that approximately 70 per cent of the increase in costs during this period arose from the rising prices of the resources – mostly human – that colleges and universities use.[6] They reached this conclusion by comparing the higher-education price index (HEPI) to the price index for goods and services in the domestic economy (the implicit-price-deflator in the gross domestic product [GDP]). Faculty salaries rose rapidly, more than offsetting a relatively small increase in average class size.

Getz and Siegfried also found that institutions had found substitutes for full-time faculty members – such as the use of more part-time and larger classes – thereby alleviating pressure on costs.[7] The investigators also looked at potential economies of scale – whether overall average costs fall as the institution grows – but found little, if any evidence of such economies, at least for institutions of similar types. They also inferred that students and their parents do, in fact, seek quality and that the observed increases in costs reflect institutional efforts to improve quality. Expenditures in categories linked to quality – student services, for example – rose rapidly relative to other categories. Finally, costs per student have tended to drop when colleges were growing and to rise when they have shrunk. Thus places with enrolment problems are likely to face increasing costs per student, creating a kind of vicious circle.

Unfortunately, no recent study uses comparable methods, so we cannot attempt the same analysis for the last decade. However, we offer some observations. First, the pattern of more rapidly growing prices for resources appears to have continued, although with smaller divergence from prices in general. In the study by Getz and Siegfried, the difference in growth between the HEPI and the GDP's implicit-price deflator was 2.0 points per year, which accounted for 70 per cent of the increase in overall costs. Between 1990 and 1998, the average difference between the two indices was 1.3 points per year. This accounts for considerably less of the increase in expenditures per student – perhaps 25 per cent, instead of Getz and Siegfried's 70 per cent.[8] Thus recent cost increases appear to have resulted more from greater use of resources of all kinds than from price inflation specific to resources in higher education.

At the same time, some of the adjustments noted by Getz and Siegfried continue. In particular, substitution of part-time for full-time members of faculty has continued apace. In the autumn of 1987, about 66 per cent of faculty members worked full time; by 1995, the figure had dropped to 59 per cent.[9] Press reports suggest that this trend is continuing.

What about technology? A dozen or so years ago, hopes were high that new technology would cut costs by increasing the productivity of the faculty and the administration alike. Data to test this idea are not available, partly because the real costs of technology are spread across many of the traditional accounting categories in academe – technology involves much more than workstations or software. Earlier hopes for technology have not been realized and probably will not be in the near future.

Yet the cost of information technology systems increases continuously, even though costs of processing power plummet in accordance with Moore's law – that computing speed doubles roughly every eighteen months. In fact, costs associated with new technology should continue to rise, both in absolute terms and as a proportion of budgets. Part of this reflects the increasing value of information systems to their users as more members of the organization use them – so-called network effects. This means that demand for systems grows continuously – there is an upward shift in demand, not merely greater quantity demanded because of lower price per unit of processing power. The increase in demand implies that the systems are valuable to users and institutions, but it is not clear how to determine this value or how it translates into revenues for the institution.

So network effects produce higher expenditures for equipment and software. But the rapid pace of technological change (Moore's law again) makes life cycles short for information technology. In turn, replacement of equipment is a large and rising cost, especially if coupled with the expanding universe of users.[10]

Further, staff costs remain constant. Staffs dealing with information technology grow as usage and demand for support expand. Also, even though sources (including the internet) are beginning to replace printed books and journals as library resources, library staffs are not shrinking. Support for printed materials is still necessary, as well as, increasingly, support for use of technological information. Also, economies in faculty size or usage have not followed, partly because bandwidths for transmission do not allow seamless remote learning.

Breakthroughs are in sight, however, although cost of access may block their adoption by small colleges.

In summary, it seems that the recent spectacular advances in information technology have not reduced costs for colleges. Indeed, the net effect has probably been to increase costs – while possibly improving the instructional process. Colleges and universities appear to have continued to economize by substituting part-time for full-time members of faculty. Price inflation for resources has been greater than that for goods and services in general, but the disparity seems smaller, because costs have risen more from purchase of greater quantities of resources than from increased prices.

Thus pressures on costs continue, but from different directions. What do these changes mean for small private colleges, like my own?

SUBSIDIES, COST CONTROL, AND VALUE FOR MONEY

As we saw at the outset, costs of educating students in American colleges exceed what they pay. The difference is a subsidy provided from other sources – Winston's "donative resources." Each institution posts a tuition fee, the so-called sticker price. The difference between this price and the average cost of education is a general subsidy, which every student enjoys. However, many, if not most, students pay less than the sticker price. The difference represents student aid, which may be disbursed on the basis of need, of merit, or of some combination of these. Call this the "individual subsidy."

Colleges are free to set their sticker prices wherever they wish; competitive forces and external pressures dictate how that price is set. The recent pressure to control "costs" apparently slowed the rate of increase of tuition fees; some schools have drastically cut fees. Has the rate of increase in costs moderated? Not necessarily; we do not yet have adequate data. If tuition fees have increased more slowly than costs, the general subsidy has gone up – a regressive step vis-à-vis equity. That scenario is consistent with the recent increased drive to raise money for endowments, student aid, and the like.

The subsidy helps explain colleges' behaviour and the steps to survival.

Cost control is certainly an option, though highly problematic. First, much of the reason for increased costs is competition. Light teaching loads, smaller classes, lower faculty–student ratios, faculty clubs, more student amenities (student unions, new and attractive buildings, better food, and so on) are the very stuff of competing for students and faculty members. As we saw above, available data hint that such competition has driven costs during the last decade. Similar points pertain to use of information technology.

But a second major factor inhibiting cost control has to do with colleges' non-profit status. What is their incentive to control costs? Who benefits? The college has to cover costs, at least over the longer run, in order to survive. But it can almost always foresee raising the funds to balance the ledger. Meanwhile, most people associated with the college benefit from more spending. Everybody likes good food and attractive buildings. All faculty members prefer light over heavy teaching loads, and they all enjoy a good faculty club. Administrators prefer to pay high salaries; it eases recruitment of personnel, and it makes life easier once the people are on board.

The one group that might have incentive to control costs is the board of trustees. Even there, the beauty of a campus, the reputation of its faculty, the quality of the students, and even fine food confer benefits on the trustees. Moreover, in most cases, trustees serve part time and have relatively limited knowledge of the institution and many demands on their time. The costs of their monitoring the administration and its decisions are high. While their intentions may be and often are of the best, they cannot readily control costs.

None of this is to say that cost control is unimportant. It's just difficult to design and impose really effective costs controls in a non-profit institution functioning in a highly competitive situation.

What other strategy for survival is there? Attention naturally must turn to what the institution offers to its constituents – mostly to students. In a paper on the competitive threat posed by proprietary institutions, Gordon Winston points to the need to offer something that justifies the difference between the price of taking courses from the proprietary university and the net price at a private, non-profit college.[11] The larger the difference, the more likely it is that the college will lose out.

This finding has two implications. First, the size of the subsidy is clearly critical, and hence the procurement of donative resources. Thus the new competition from the private sector (and from programs offered on the internet by traditional institutions) creates a powerful new incentive to raise funds. Other things being equal, the larger the subsidy (general plus average individual), the harder it is for the for-profit institution to compete. Second, any remaining difference must be justifiable to potential students (or their parents) in terms of additional benefits provided. Private colleges must provide educational experiences different from competitors, as well as services that students value. Hence the rush to provide ever more-elaborate activity centres, overseas travel programs, and the like. In the for-profit sector, cutting costs is one important response to competition – note – recent "down-sizing" and other cost-controlling measures. But in the non-profit sector of higher education, competition may actually drive up costs, as competitors strive to provide the extra quality needed for survival.

CONCLUSION

All of this puts small colleges in especially difficult positions. Often working on tight budgets, they cannot easily find the resources required to provide the "competitive edge." It seems to me that it will pose a greater challenge for them than for large institutions because of the economies of scale in that area and because of positive network effects related directly to size. Clearly, we must be able to offer value that justifies our higher cost (this pertains not only to the proprietary institutions, but also to the public institutions with which we compete). This value may be the residential nature of the college. It may be the positive interactions of students in a residential setting. It may be a religious bent. It may be in the quality of the faculty. Whatever it is, the college must identify the factors that separate it from other institutions, add value, and do so at relatively low cost.

NOTES

1 National Commission on the Cost of Higher Education, *Straight Talk about College Costs and Prices*, 21 Jan. 1998.
2 See, for example, "College Tuition Outpaces Inflation Again," *Wall Street Journal*, 12 March 1999.
3 Gordon C. Winston, Jared C. Carbone, and Ethan G. Lewis, "What's Been Happening to Higher Education? A Reference Manual," Williams Project on the Economics of Higher Education, Williamstown, Mass.,

March 1999. Calculation of the percentages factors in an estimate of capital costs, which college accounts rarely include.

4 *Chronicle of Higher Education*, 12 May 2000, A40–44. The other closings were at the Ambassador University (Texas), Phillips University (Oklahoma), Sue Bennett College (Kentucky), University of Central Texas, and Westmar University (Iowa).

5 Malcolm Getz and John J. Siegfried, "Costs and Productivity in American Colleges and Universities," in Charles T. Clotfelter et al., *Economic Challenges in Higher Education* (Chicago: University of Chicago Press, 1991), 261–392.

6 Ibid., 300.

7 Ibid., 391.

8 Getz and Siegfried adjusted HEGIS/IPEDS data to estimate adjusted educational and general (E&G) expenditures per student. The "rough" estimate above uses E&G and enrolment data from the 1999 *Digest of Education Statistics*. I made no effort to adjust these data.

9 Ibid., Table 230.

10 Given the short life cycles, policies for buying computer equipment differ from those for most capital goods. See John L. Oberlin, "The Financial Mythology of Information Technology: Developing a New Game Plan," *Cause/Effect* (summer 1996), 10–17.

11 Gordon C. Winston, "For-profit Higher Education: Godzilla or Chicken Little," Williams Project for the Economics of Higher Education, ms., Nov. 1998.

The Challenge to the Traditional College by the For-profit College

STEPHEN R. GREENWALD

The rapid growth of for-profit higher education in the United States and elsewhere raises significant issues for private, not-for-profit colleges and universities and for higher education generally. The for-profit sector, which targets primarily working adults, has been taking a consistently larger share of the market for bachelor's and master's degrees in the last decade.[1] The University of Phoenix, now the largest U.S. private university, has over 70,000 full-time students and is growing by 20 per cent each year.[2] The for-profit phenomenon raises issues about the role and goals of higher education and about the viability and relevance of traditional models. The competitive challenge is real: the president of the University of Phoenix has publicly predicted the demise of many non-elite, especially private, traditional academic institutions because of their inability to meet market demands fuelling the for-profit sector.[3]

As president of a smaller non-for-profit (Audrey Cohen College in New York, with 1,500 full-time students, most of them working adults), I have been considering the likely effects of the for-profits' growth on my institution and on not-for-profits generally. I address some of those implications and a few of the issues raised by these developments that I believe those responsible for traditional institutions cannot afford to ignore.

I believe that not-for-profit colleges and universities play a vital role that for-profit institutions cannot duplicate. But the challenges are real and must be met.

The first section briefly sketches and seeks to explain the growth of the for-profit sector. The second suggests the major distinctions between it and traditional not-for-profits. The third lays out some of the challenges posed by the for-profits. The fourth addresses the continuing strengths of the not-for-profit sector, and the fifth proposes some changes.

GROWTH OF THE FOR-PROFIT SECTOR

The for-profit sector has expanded rapidly of late, fuelled by market demand and by information technology (IT). One estimate finds about 600 for-profit institutions in the United States; the University of Phoenix, a subsidiary of the Apollo Group, a public company, is by far the largest.[4] Other major players include:

- DeVry, Inc., which operates the DeVry Institutes
- Jones International University, a fully accredited, "virtual" on-line university
- Kaplan, Inc., a subsidiary of the Washington Post Company, which has formed an on-line law school and other ventures in higher education, including acquiring Quest Education Corporation, a chain of colleges in eleven U.S. states
- North Anglica Education PLC, which owns the School of Finance and Management in the United Kingdom
- Sylvan Learning Systems, a public company acquiring colleges and universities in the United States and Europe
- the Whitman Education Group, Inc., operator of twenty-four proprietary colleges in thirteen U.S. states

An analogous development is the proliferation of "corporate universities" – in-house training and educational facilities run by companies for their employees. One current estimate has about 6,000 operating in the United States.[5]

The University of Phoenix was started about thirty years ago but grew most rapidly in the last decade. Other for-profits, such as DeVry, Jones International, Kaplan, and Sylvan Learning, started or expanded significantly in recent years.

What accounts for the recent growth? First, a significant shift occurred to older, working adults. Today, students twenty-five and older make up 40 per cent of enrolment in U.S. higher education.[6]

Their interests and needs differ from those of "traditional" students eighteen to twenty-three years old, the for-profit sector has zeroed in on them and done a better job of satisfying them.

Second, a transformation in the nature of work has taken place, with more jobs requiring managerial, technical, and professional training and certification. The for-profits, unencumbered by traditional curriculum and faculty structures, have tailored degree and certificate programs to the needs of corporate employers, sometimes in collaboration with them.[7]

Third, use of technology has grown rapidly in higher education, via on-line delivery of curriculum. The for-profit sector, free from traditional structures, and supported by equity and debt capital raised in the public or private markets, made the necessary investments and quickly established capability in distance learning. The University of Phoenix, for example, now has about 11,000 on-line students, and all the for-profits offer on-line programs.[8] Some, like Jones University and Kaplan's law school, are "virtual" schools, entirely on-line.

Fourth, distance learning is particularly appealing to working adult learners, who make up a growing proportion of the college market, helping to expand the for-profit sector. Smaller not-for-profits, such as my institution, compete in the same market but have fewer resources and no access to investment capital for developing on-line capability.

DISTINCTIONS BETWEEN FOR-PROFITS NOT-FOR-PROFITS

For-profit and not-for-profit colleges obviously have much in common. All are subject to state, regional, and/or national accreditation standards and review.[9] They thus have similar requirements in terms of minimum curriculum content, credit hours, and so on required for degrees. And, institutions in both sectors market themselves in similar ways, now including extensive use of the internet and websites. Tuition fees do not differ radically between the sectors, with rates per credit hour falling in the same range.

But there are major differences in five areas examined in this section – philosophy, curriculum design and delivery, delivery of services, faculty structure, and resource allocation. Each of these distinctions poses a challenge to the not-for-profits, particularly to those competing with the for-profit sector. The challenge for a not-for-profit is to defend traditional practices on grounds that are intellectually and/or economically sound or to recognize a better approach and adopt it in a way consistent with the institution's values, mission, and resources.

Philosophically, for-profits view higher education almost exclusively through an instrumental, utilitarian lens. They focus relentlessly on "vocationalism."[10] Their curriculum usually reflects this view by minimizing course work outside the vocational career track chosen by the student. The president of a for-profit college in Florida stated: "We're not teaching the Great Books to the elites; we're appealing to more middle class students who want a focused, practical education."[11]

Obviously all institutions of higher education seek to equip students to succeed in their work and careers. However, most not-for-profits have a wider mission.

Another vital fact about for-profit colleges is precisely that they are "for profit"; their ultimate purpose is to generate profits for their owners. Educating people is instrumental wholly to the goal of making money. Again, there is nothing wrong with making a profit. Those in the for-profit sector would argue that the search for profit encourages efficiency and discourages waste. I suggest, however, that the ultimate goal of profit will on occasion supersede an institution's mission, or at least some part of it. I believe that this distinction in ultimate purposes explains many of the critical differences between the two sectors. In health care, similar, but much more expansive, "profitization" has raised disturbing questions about quality of service.[12]

The for-profit approach directly affects design and development of programs and curricula. Unlike traditional not-for-profits, where curriculum is the province mainly of the faculty, most for-profits develop it centrally, and it is entirely prescriptive. Every course is taught from a syllabus designed by a "subject-matter expert," often in consultation with outside employers.[13] The teacher's job is to deliver the prescribed course content as written. This approach follows logically from the model of vocationalism, which expects students to acquire a specified set of prescribed skills.

Besides keeping them out of curriculum design, for-profits exclude faculty members from making assessments, using instead standard forms of testing. Jorge Klor de Alva, president of the University of

Phoenix, has spoken of "unbundling" faculty roles, in response to demand for "student driven" curriculum and educational "account-ability."[14] The traditional model, as practised in most not-for-profits, is supposedly unresponsive to those demands, with institutions unwilling to address the needs of students or to accept independent assessment of "outcomes."

For-profit colleges and universities overwhelmingly use part-time faculty members. The University of Phoenix – again representative – employs about 100 full-timers out of a total of more than 6,500. At a symposium at Audrey Cohen College, Klor de Alva questioned the need for any full-time people on faculty, asserting that academically qualified "practitioners" are, after a five-week training course, equal if not superior in teaching ability.[15] This almost-total reliance on part-time "practitioners" follows from the vocational model, where "prac-tical" and "focused" education is the gold standard.

Contrast this model with the not-for-profit sector. While traditional institutions increasingly use adjunct instructors, full-times still teach the bulk of a curriculum, certainly at the undergraduate level and in general education programs. The president of one not-for-profit col-lege recently wrote that "teaching 40, 50, or even 60 percent of our sections with part-time faculty is pretty much academically indefen-sible."[16] How can we reconcile these starkly different views?

Student or "customer" service differs radically in the two sectors. Besides offering a greet deal of distance learning, for-profits tailor delivery to working adults. Most classes take place year round, on evenings and weekends. Scheduling is quite flexible, with students at Phoenix, for example, taking courses sequentially, one at a time. While some not-for-profits that cater to the same population, such as my institution, have some similar approaches to delivery, many do not. For-profit institutions are more market-driven, tending to see students as customers and to deal with them on those terms, allocat-ing substantial financial and human resources to acquiring and then retaining students. Older, working adults, many of them profession-als, have limited time to deal with admissions, registration, financial aid, payment, records acquisition, and so on and are generally less tolerant of inefficient service than younger students. Klor de Alva observes that (the students) "want their needs to be anticipated, immediately addressed, and courteously handled. They do not want to wait, stand in line, deal with inefficient bureaucrats, or be treated like petitioning intruders rather than valued customers."[18]

He adds that traditional institutions find it "nearly impossible" to meet these needs. While I disagree, I do know from my own experience and observations that some not-for-profits perceive students, if not as "petitioning intruders," then as supplicants, rather as than customers with other options. Since the working-adult segment of the student population is growing rapidly, not-for-profits competing for those students need to address these issues.

Practices differ also in resource allocation. For-profit institutions invest very little in physical plant, and most have no library facilities, relying on on-line databases. Classes are taught in leased facilities, and most for-profits need few of the support facilities customary at more traditional institutions.[17] Clearly, as I suggested above, for-profits invest less in the full-time faculty and have moved more quickly into it.

CHALLENGES

I want now to narrow the focus of our inquiry. First, I do not believe that this is an either or issue. There is room, and need enough, for a broad variety of institutions. No one set of institutions or model of education can meet today's complex needs.

Second, the challenges posed by growth of the for-profit sector do not fall equally on all not-for-profit colleges. For-profit institutions do not threaten the well-entrenched, well-endowed "elite" private universities (both large and small) and the larger public universities. The universities have substantial resources, play too critical a role, and will continue to attract their share of students. Nor do they compete directly with the for-profits in the marketplace. Although many have substantial adult-education extension programs, directed towards working adults, these operations are not at the core of what they do.

Rather, smaller, less well-endowed institutions, both private and public, including many community colleges, are more directly in the for-profits' line of fire. If for-profit advocates are right, and future students demand the "practical, focused, flexible, student-driven, vocational" type of education offered by the for-profits, then, as Klor de Alva has predicted, many non-elite traditional institutions may not survive. Does that matter? Should these institutions be saved? Is there any reason for their survival if they cannot meet these market demands? I believe that the answer is yes and discuss why below.

The better-entrenched institutions, however, still face challenges. The for-profit phenomenon, in my view, poses two sets of challenges that I consider in this section. The first, suggested above, more directly affects smaller institutions. The second, involving factors external to institutions, is more indirect and subtle, raising issues about the proper role of higher education. To the extent that the for-profit model appears to respond better to current demands, it will call into question assumptions about the proper goals of higher education, about how to meet those goals, and about how to allocate resources, including public funds. This could affect the entire not-for-profit sector.

As for the first set of direct challenges, I set out above some of the major differences between the two sectors. I claimed that these differences may force not-for-profits either to defend traditional practice or to move towards the for-profit approach. Although resolving that issue is beyond the scope of this paper, I suggest a possible direction for responses.

Not-for-profit institutions should have missions that go far beyond the narrow vocationalism of most for-profits. The challenge is to better explain and justify that mission to students and to the wider public. There is some real danger in profit's being the ultimate purpose of for-profits, with the public good only instrumental to that purpose.

As to design and control of program and curriculum, having a wholly prescriptive curriculum designed by a central authority reduces teachers to delivery instruments. Uniform curriculum content is entirely appropriate in some program areas, particularly in scientific and technical fields, including information management and computer technology, and in professional studies such as engineering and accounting. The danger lies in pushing that concept too far – into business management, human services, human resource management, psychology, and particularly the liberal arts and humanities. While the for-profits concentrate on professional studies, this approach ill-serves their many programs in "softer" fields.[19]

The centrally designed curriculum and the "unbundling" of faculty roles represent a search for cost effectiveness. For-profit advocates constantly harp on "ineffective decision making processes" in the traditional sector, attributable mainly to faculty control over curriculum, scheduling, assessment, and the like. This "ineffectiveness" allegedly keeps institutions from responding properly to "market" demands, although I have yet to see any empirical data to support that claim. Certainly, the messy processes of the traditional academy vex all of us at times, but the faculty's autonomy and its control over the central components of learning are at the core of a system of higher education that has served Western societies well for centuries. In contrast, centralized control over curriculum and assessment, coupled with extensive use of part-timers, merely saves money – but at what cost?

Obviously not-for-profits can and should strive to be cost-effective, but not by sacrificing sound pedagogy. Their challenge, again, is to explain to students and the public why their model is sound and to maintain sufficient flexibility to makes changes when and if appropriate. For example, within the traditional academy, issues such as faculty tenure and the proper allocation of faculty members' time, particularly vis-à-vis teaching, have been subjects of debate for some time, and change has been and is taking place.[20] This is as it should be.

For-profits' almost-exclusive use of part-timers poses a multifaceted challenge to not-for-profits. Clearly, part-timers play a major role in all institutions. Use of working professionals with expertise and experience is quite appropriate in certain programs, especially professional and graduate studies. So for-profits' emphasis on professional studies may justify their disproportionate use of part-timers. Yet many not-for-profits that also offer professional studies, such as my institution, have adjuncts teaching a much lower proportion of course content and, as in our case, plan to lower that percentage even further.

Again, I believe that the issues concerning part-timers relate to the basic differences between the two-sectors. As with "unbundling," the prime impulse involves cost and profits. A competent full-time academician brings a dimension to teaching that no part-time "practitioner" can. The teacher's broad understanding of the entire curriculum and academic area, and his or her ongoing scholarship, allow him or her to fit the course content firmly within, and relate it to, the entire program and to help students acquire and use the skills of critical thinking and reasoning basic to creative, higher-order intellectual achievement.

If I am right, that is a model worth defending. That model, however, is less "efficient," and for-profits may find the efficiency promised by the alternative quite tempting. This could be particularly challenging to public institutions dependent on state funding, although trustees of private colleges are also more and more cost-conscious.

Klor de Alva frequently refers to a 1998 poll of fifty state governors conducted by the Education Commission of the States. The governors judged four items to be of least importance:

- maintaining faculty authority for curriculum content, quality, and degree requirements
- preserving the present balance of faculty research, teaching load, and community service
- ensuring a campus-based experience for the majority of students
- maintaining traditional faculty roles and tenure[21]

While the poll does not necessarily mean that cost considerations underlay the priority rankings, it certainly does indicate that when state governments allocate resources to higher education, full-timers' salaries and benefits will not be high on their list.

The not-for-profits must defend full-timers to students, policy-makers and the public, while remaining open and flexible about reasonable changes in faculty structure.

As for curriculum delivery, particularly distance learning, IT is here to stay, and not-for-profits must figure out how to use it in ways consistent with their missions and values. For-profits have been quicker to take advantage of such systems, and in the market of working adult learners, the efficiencies offered by on-line learning have great appeal. Also, the challenge is pedagogical; technology, properly deployed, can enhance learning.

The issue of technology raises another challenge, and possible danger, for not-for-profits. In just the past few years, several large colleges and universities have moved into distance learning via for-profit subsidiaries or joint ventures with for-profits. Some faculty members now want a "piece of the action."[22]

Not-for-profits may try to emulate for-profits with for-profit on-line learning, more part-timers, and centralized curriculum design and control, without thinking through the implications of such practices.

Institutions anxious to attract working adults will need more flexibility in scheduling, offering more courses on evenings and weekends and year round. This may, of course, raise problems with the faculty.

For-profits now seem to offer the best student or customer service. This poses a distinct challenge to not-for-profits competing for working adult students, who have, and will exercise, other options, including choosing a for-profit college, if their needs and expectations about service are not met. Enhancing service delivery will require cultural and attitudinal changes among college administrators and staff, as well as greater use of management information system (MIS) technology.

The challenges for the wider not-for-profit sector are less direct. I have proposed continued support for the role of full-time members of faculty. This issue, however, implicates a larger one about the continuing relevance of the traditional not-for-profit institution's mission, which goes beyond the narrow vocationalism of for-profit institutions.

In the survey of governors mentioned above, the four items ranked lowest represent practices pretty much jettisoned by the for-profits. In contrast, the for-profits embrace the four items ranked highest – lifelong learning, technology and distance learning, collaboration with business in curriculum and program development, and integrating applied or on-the-job experience into academic programs. This alignment of governors and for-profits may not be coincidental. The for-profit community has a better sense of the views of policymakers and of how to respond. And the views of business leaders would probably track those of the governors.

The views of these critical constituencies may threaten continued financial and other support for non-profits. Indeed, the chair of the Massachusetts Board of Higher Education, reacting to the University of Phoenix's application to enter that state, observed about the for-profit model: "I'd like to see this stuff in all institutions in Massachusetts. My prayer would be that state institutions would take a damn hard look at this stuff and say, 'Let's do some of this stuff. Let's do a lot of this stuff.'"[23]

The for-profit sector has grown rapidly, particularly among working professionals. That expansion indicates that fewer and fewer people in their twenties and thirties see the need for, or relevance of, a non-vocational college education. For many of them, a broader, more traditional institution is not what they need or want. But many who make that choice might well benefit from a more traditional higher education, and the not-for-profits should try to convince them of why that might be the case.

In a further, indirect challenge posed by the for-profit model, certification and alternative forms of "credentialling" are replacing college degree programs. Until recently, outside of trade guilds and professional licensing bodies, colleges and universities had a new-monopoly on tertiary credentials. That has changed, however, particularly in IT, which has given rise to an enormous, unregulated for-profit training and credentialling industry.[24] This industry is unregulated by public authorities, including accreditation bodies. Accreditation comes from corporations in the IT industry, such as Cisco, Microsoft, and Oracle. Many other fields have seen a proliferation of non-accredited programs, many offered by accredited institutions. The corporate accreditation model may well be extended to other areas of learning. Coupled with the emergence of corporate universities, this trend indicates to me further entrenchment of a vocationalist approach to postsecondary education. The growth of these alternative models – less expensive, more accessible, and less time-consuming – raises further questions about traditional education.

For-profits may have easier access to alternative financing sources and other benefits. We must, however, weigh their access to public and private equity and debt markets against the not-for-profits' ability to raise funds through tax-deductible contributions. Both sources of financing have benefited of late from the surging economy and stock markets, and availability would probably stay in tandem if the markets move either up or down. However, smaller, less well-endowed institutions probably have less access to funding. Some institutions have explored innovative ways to create "for-profit" subsidiaries or ventures in order to raise capital.[25] As I suggested above, these ventures may prove troublesome.

A for-profit institution can also offer stock to members of staff and faculty. During boom times this can be a powerful magnet, drawing talent away from not-for-profits. Colleagues cashing in on profit opportunities may, however, stir discontent in the faculty and the staff.[26]

NOT-FOR-PROFITS' STRENGTHS

During a recent conversation I asked a colleague why any private college or university should remain not for profit. Outside its ability to solicit tax-deductible contributions (which a for-profit's access to capital may more than offset), why should a not-for-profit remain so?

The answer, I think, goes to the very heart of the not-for-profit's *raison d'être*.

For-profit institutions have a major role to play, offering a highly focused, practical, vocationalist sort of higher education that suits many students. However, I do believe that some of the claims made by for-profit advocates – that thesis is a better way to meet today's needs – are overblown and misleading. So too are their justifications for certain of their academic practices, which seem to aim at generating profits. The not-for-profit sector, beset by many other challenges, has been slow to defend itself.

Some for-profits' disdain for traditional education is condescending towards their own students. Dismissal of "great books" as being only for "elites," and claims that "middle-class" students need only a "practical" education, bespeak an attitude that in effect denies those students any higher aspirations. Not for them are public or community service, creative endeavours, or the broader grasp of knowledge required at the highest levels of business and society.

The very concept "not-for-profit" implies a purpose beyond commercial gain. Institutions are not for profit, and enjoy the benefits of that status, because their ultimate purpose is to improve the common weal, to create public goods that benefit society in general. In the case of higher education, one of those goods is certainly graduates who have acquired skills sufficient to engage in productive work, to support themselves and their families. But higher education also fulfils other roles, which do not translate as easily into economic gain, but are crucial to civic society and culture. Not-for-profit institutions can, and do, fill these roles.

They produce aware, informed, and engaged citizens through education in civics, history, values, and ethics. Political participation, for instance, is greater among college graduates than among nongraduates, although we must do better, but facilitating it is one of the roles that higher education should play and that for-profits cannot and will not.

Another is to empower students to be leaders and agents for positive change in their lives, careers, and communities. This requires an education that goes beyond the vocational and provides a basic understanding of society and culture, equipping the student with higher-order skills of creativity, critical thinking, and communication and with the ability to link concepts and ideas from different fields and disciplines. These are the skills that leadership requires and that a broadly based education with a significant component of liberal arts and humanities can provide.

Not-for-profit institutions are also vehicles for social mobility and socialization, especially for those at the lowest rungs of society. My own institution, Audrey Cohen College, in my view exemplifies this role. Almost 90 per cent of our students are people of colour, with an average age of thirty-two and average annual family income in the low $20,000s. Many entering students lack basic learning skills, as well as skills to manoeuvre in the world of work. Much of what we, and particularly our full-time faculty members, do aims to equip students with basic learning and social skills. All our graduates have gone on to productive careers in human services and business, and hundreds have become leaders in their professions and communities. For-profit institutions are not prepared, or equipped, to play this role.

Historically, colleges and universities have also been repositories of knowledge and centres of debate and discussion about social issues. These are not roles that will be filled by for-profit institutions.

I am sure that one can think of other critical functions and roles that not-for-profit institutions perform and that the for-profit sector will not. Again, I do not mean to be critical of the for-profits; their missions do not include providing civic education, empowerment for social and community leadership, and upward social mobility and socialization or serving as centres for debate, discussion, and ideas and as repositories of knowledge. Nor are they organized or staffed to carry out these functions.

As I said above, for-profits pose a direct and immediate challenge to the smaller, non-elite, private and public institutions, many located in urban environments, that compete with the for-profits in the marketplace. These not-for-profits perform the critical functions outlined above, and they do so for many who do not have access to the large, or more elite institutions. If Klor de Alva is right, and many of these smaller institutions do not survive and are replaced by for-profits, then their constituencies will be cut off from an education that could enable many of them to become social, political, and business leaders. That, in my view, would be a severe loss for our society.

RESPONSES TO FOR-PROFIT CHALLENGES

Throughout this paper I have suggested ways in which the not-for-profit sector could respond to the for-profit model. Here I summarize a few of the most important.

First, not-for-profits must better articulate and defend what they do. Prospective students should understand their educational choices and the trade-offs between competing models of learning. Many will still choose the flexibility, focus, and practicality of a for-profit institution, but many will not, if they understand what they may be giving up.

I quoted above the chair of the Massachusetts Board of Higher Education. Perhaps policy and business leaders, if better informed, might hesitate before pressing traditional institutions to become more like for-profits, de-emphasizing or abandoning academic structures that have developed over centuries.

Second, the not-for-profit sector should look at what the for-profits do well, particularly in customer service, and emulate those practices where possible. I keep expounding this theme at Audrey Cohen College. In 1964, when the college started, very few institutions in New York were serving working adults. Now, almost all institutions, including Columbia University and New York University, are pursuing adult learners. Competition is fierce, students have many more choices, and customer service affects their decisions. In speaking with recent graduates of Audrey Cohen, I learned that, while most were very satisfied, many were unhappy about how the "system" treated them and so are reluctant to recommend the college to others. As a result, I have looked at ways in which for-profits and other institutions offer student services and have improved what we do. Part of this process involves changing employees' attitudes, so that they perceive students as intelligent consumers with choices. It is not easy, but we are getting better.

Third, not-for-profits must adapt technology to both teaching and administration rapidly and responsively, consistent with their resources, and with the faculty's co-operation and involvement. This too will not be easy and will require substantial resources, but it is essential, particularly for institutions competing for the working adult learner.

Fourth, not-for-profit colleges should not abandon the structures and systems that give them their character. Attempts to become more like for-profits and to compete on their terms will, in my opinion, fail. The for-profits do what they do well and are generally better financed than the smaller, non-elite non-profits.

Finally, I believe strongly that the very fundamental difference in ultimate purposes between the two sectors has real meaning and needs to be more widely discussed. It does matter whether an institution's final accountability is to its owners or to its students. The health-care analogy should raise concerns about any substantial shift to the for-profit model in higher education.

NOTES

1 Katherine S. Mangan, "More Enroll in Business at For-profit Colleges," *Chronicle of Higher Education*, 1 Oct. 1999, A54, noting that business degrees awarded by for-profits jumped 180 per cent between 1992 and 1997.
2 *Newsweek*, 10 Jan. 2000, 138.
3 Jorge Klor de Alva, "Remaking the Academy," *Educause* (March/April 2000), 32–40.
4 Remarks of Frank Newman, delivered at a symposium of the American Association of Community Colleges (AACC) held at Audrey Cohen College (ACC), 2 June 2000. I am indebted to Drs Jorge Klor de Alva, Robin McClintock, Frank Newman, and Alan Wolfe, who participated in the symposium, for their stimulating ideas, many of which informed the ideas in this paper.
5 Remarks of Jorge Klor de Alva, AACC Symposium
6 David Marcus, "A Scholastic Gold Mine," *U.S. News & World Report*, 24 Jan. 2000, 44.
7 Jorge Klor de Alva has stated that "a real and perceived skill mismatch exists between the needs of the workplace and traditional education." ACC symposium, June 2000.
8 Karen W. Arenson, "Going Higher Tech Degree by Degree," *New York Times*, 1 Jan. 2000, 29.
9 The introduction and proliferation of on-line programs have generated controversy in the accreditation field, and some traditionalists are charging that accrediting agencies are weakening standards to accommodate the trend. See Florence Olsen, "Virtual Institutions Challenge Accreditors to Devise New Ways of Measuring Quality," *Chronicle of Higher Education*, 6 Aug. 1999, A29.
10 William H. Honan, "Timid at the Top: A Question of Leadership," *New York Times*, 26 Jan. 2000, B8. Honan refers to for-profits as "McUniversities."
11 Marcus, "Gold Mine," quoting Arthur Keiser, founder of Keiser College.
12 Arthur Levine, president of Teachers College, Columbia University, reports that a corporate entrepreneur recently told him, "You're going

to be the next health care: a poorly managed/non-profit industry which was overtaken by the profit-making sector." Arthur Levine, "The Soul of a New University," *New York Times*, 13 March 2000. Some would say that this prospect is cause for alarm, not cheer.

13 Klor de Alva, "Remaking the Academy," 37.

14 Remarks at ACC symposium.

15 Remarks at ACC symposium.

16 Fulton, "The Plight of Part-timers in Higher Education," *Change* (May/June 2000), 39–43. On the shift to part-timers, see "Part-timers Continue to Replace Full-timers on College Faculties," *Chronicle of Higher Education*, 28 Jan. 2000.

17 The lack of library facilities can affect nearby institutions. The dean of the University of New Orleans Metropolitan College noted: "I compete with the University of Phoenix. They don't bother me, but their students show up at our library and that's an expense to the state." "Colleges Warned of Rising Private Competition," *Advocate* (Baton Rouge, La.), 5 Aug. 1999, 18-A.

18 Klor de Alva, *Newsweek*, 10 Jan. 2000.

19 For example, the University of Phoenix offers programs and degrees in business administration, counselling, education, general studies, health care services, human services, management, marketing, and organizational leadership.

20 "Report Urges Post-Tenure Reviews for Professors," *Chronicle of Higher Education*, 22 Jan. 1999; Nelson, "The War against the Faculty," *Chronicle of Higher Education*, 16 April 1999, B4.

21 Klor de Alva, *Newsweek*, 10 Jan. 2000, citing the Education Commission of the States, *Transforming Post-secondary Education for the Twenty-first Century: View of the Governors* (June 1998).

22 Steinberg and Wyatt, "Boola, Boola: e-Commerce Comes to the Quad," *New York Times*, 13 Feb. 2000. See also Goldstein, "Capital Ideas," *University Business*, 1 Oct. 1999, 46–52.

23 Zernile, "Arizona-Based For-profit College Gets Warm Reception in Massachusetts," *Boston Globe*, 19 May 1999.

24 Adelman, "Parallel Universe, Certification in the Information-Technology Guild," *Change* (May/June 2000), 20.

25 Goldstein, "Capital Ideas."

26 Steinberg and Wyatt, "Boola, Boola."

Back to Earth:
Expectations for Using
Technology to Improve
the University Experience

DAVID W. OLIEN

Some observers have suggested that traditional universities will in the new century give way to virtual universities located in cyberspace. I do not see such an extreme change occurring. The heritage and reputation so exemplified by the colleges at Oxford and Cambridge, combined with the strength of quality institutions around the globe, argue against that happening. Still, we should aim neither too high, with out-of-this-world expectations about what the new technology can accomplish, or so low that we miss an opportunity to improve education. I would like to bring expectations back to earth, while embracing exciting possibilities for change.

We are in the greatest age of change in telecommunications since the beginning of the industrial revolution. Technology is bringing advances to communications in ways not imaginable just a few years ago. It is impossible to miss the changes as you read the daily newspapers in almost any nation.

Earlier in the twentieth century, telegraph, telephone, radio, and television communications affected mostly consumers' choices. While telegraph and telephone enabled news to travel more quickly and permitted long-distance investment decisions, radio and television served basically as media for communication, entertainment, and attempts to influence consumers' choices.

Today's changes, however, particularly the emergence of the internet, have created an instantaneous global marketplace, where consumers can view competing products at competing prices. Individuals wanting to purchase a CD, for example, can visit a website, listen to samples of the music, and then order it for delivery without ever visiting a local store.

Similarly, on-line booksellers such as Amazon.com are transforming how people buy books. Consumers are also making travel arrangements, previewing real estate, and obtaining everything from prescription drugs to automobiles via the worldwide web. It is no longer particularly important whether the business is located in London or Amsterdam; in Rome, Italy, or in Rome, New York.

Communication technology will next penetrate our daily lives with the predicted convergence of digital television and the personal computer. The ability of digital television broadcast centres to transmit streams of wireless data to personal computers at speeds 700 times faster than the internet is likely to affect many aspects of our lives, including commerce and health care. It may also reshape the learning experience.

I look in turn at demand for higher education, use of information technology to increase access, limits to expansion, virtual universities versus traditional education, and technology to enhance the campus experience. Throughout I refer to the University of Wisconsin and its experience. I conclude with a series of questions about how technological change may affect students, institutions, and the creation, dissemination, and maintenance of knowledge.

DEMAND FOR HIGHER EDUCATION

Powerful forces beyond technological innovation are encouraging universities to reach out to traditional and non-traditional students to provide information and services using new information technology (IT). Political support continues to be strong for providing broad access to greater educational and, hence, better economic opportunities. There is also increased recognition that expansion and development of new knowledge help maintain and expand prosperity.

Besides improving the intellectual quality of one's life, the economic advantages offered to college-educated individuals are undeniable. In 1997, according to the U.S. Department of Commerce, individuals eighteen and older with a bachelor's degree had average annual earnings of $40,478, compared with $22,895 for those with high school diplomas. The annual difference of $17,583 turns into $703,320 over a forty-year career.

Other benefits accrue as well. Individuals with higher earnings are generally going to save more for retirement and, since retirement plans are usually based on a percentage of salary, will have higher retirement income. Further, they will invest more in real estate and other objects and activities and generate significantly more overall wealth.

The U.S. Department of Education has projected that enrolment will grow significantly, from 14.1 million students in 1997 to 16.1 million in 2007. This has put considerable pressure on U.S. public policy-makers to expand access, but attempts to do so via IT have not succeeded yet. Sobering realities have brought back to earth visions that were out of touch with both available resources and consumers' desires and preferences. Although internet technology has not increased access to higher education as greatly or as quickly as many had hoped, positive changes are occurring.

TECHNOLOGY AS A MEANS TO EXPAND ACCESS

Distance education has, of course, been part of U.S. higher education for over a century. My institution has delivered coursework by mail for well over one hundred years, as it implemented the vision of President Charles Van Hise. In 1904, he saw the campus as covering the state of Wisconsin. Educational delivery via radio and television has been under way for decades.

On the success side, IT allows public, private, non-profit, and for-profit institutions to offer courses over the internet to students throughout the world. In England, the Open University has for some time used IT to deliver quality instruction in a non-traditional manner. Many traditional institutions offer specialized degrees to targeted audiences. For example, Duke University in North Carolina offers a global MBA, and National Technological University is the world's largest grantor of master's degrees in engineering.

In 1997, the University of Wisconsin (UW) System of twenty-sic compuses established the Learning Innovations Center to develop and support on-line learning for students within and outside the state. The centre is the UW System's focal point for creating, distributing, and evaluating electronic learning products. It supports existing faculty and degree programs, eliminating the need for a separate bureaucracy. For example, when a UW campus or department wants to deliver a degree program through distance education, Learning Innovations will help conduct market research, design and develop courseware, distribute the course, copyright the materials, and provide ongoing technical support. For the student, it provides on-line course information; assessments, registration, and financial services. In the next two or three years, it will develop outsourcing partnerships to create and support a wide array of asynchronous UW educational offerings. Its learner-centered environment removes many time and place barriers.[1]

On the not-so-successful side are two high-profile projects: Western Governors University and California Virtual University. By opening Western Governors in 1998, policy-makers in several states had hoped to relieve pressures of student access in a portion of the U.S. west. The university brokers and markets courses from established colleges and also trains corporate employees, linking them to courses from publishers, software developers, and other companies that have devised employee-training plans.[2] While it offers no courses of its own, it grants associates degrees and certification. It plans to become a leader in "competence-based degrees," predicated on a student's abilities and knowledge as measured by third-party testing.[3]

However, the enterprise does not appear to be growing at a rate that will significantly reduce pressure to build or expand campuses. Although state officials and administrators still have high hopes for it, enrolment has been less than expected, estimated by some sources at 100 students or fewer.[4] For the first time, supporters are seeking federal funds ($8 million) development.[5]

California Virtual University also fell short of the promoters' vision. Some policy-makers had hoped that the university would generate income for state universities and for professors to develop distance-education courses that could be marketed and sold around the world. Officials with Governor Pete Wilson called distance education an "enormous financial opportunity for the faculty and the campuses."[6] However, just eight months after the state established California Virtual as an independent, non-profit foundation, the university folded for financial reasons.[7]

In addition to the organizational flaws and fiscal realities, virtual universities are not attracting traditional college students partly because students seeking a traditional campus experience do not see them as a substitute. Instead these institutions tend to attract non-traditional students – a large and ever-increasing market. During its existence, a spokesperson for California Virtual noted the high number of "hits" that its website received *during the workday*.[8] In May, 2000, the *Chronicle of Higher Education* profiled a "typical" student at Western Governors: thirty-one years old and computer literate, with almost no college education and no time for classes at a traditional university. This older, non-traditional student is the kind of client to whom university officials say they are catering.[9]

LIMITS TO EXPANSION OF UNDERGRADUATE PROGRAMS ON-LINE

Several years ago, our campus of the University of the Wisconsin (UW) System believed that it could quickly become a major force globally by offering a large number of on-line courses. There existed an enormous, unmet need to serve non-traditional students and to provide more continuing education. The UW System has not yet developed plans to serve all those markets, nor have peer institutions. I see three main reasons for this deliberate pace.

First, requests from faculty members for assistance in applying IT to improve the learning experience on campus have far surpassed expectations. Initially, many felt that perhaps 10 per cent of campus courses would immediately use the new technology. Instead, faculty members soon began impressive innovations in their classrooms.

A 1998 survey of faculty members revealed that nearly all of them had access to the internet from their offices. More than three-quarters were using e-mail regularly to communicate with students, and over half were using the web for coursework. Fully one-third reported using computer simulations or presentation software in the classroom. Two-thirds expressed a desire for training in IT and wanted presentation graphics, desktop publishing software, and internet tools. IT's penetration into the classroom was equally impressive: 29 per cent of faculty members had computer simulations in class, and one-quarter had course web pages. Fully 15 per cent were using commercial courseware, while nearly an equal percentage had personally developed courseware.

Second, capital costs have inhibited provision of a large number of on-line programs. Capital is required to pay for hardware; working capital is necessary to finance course development, student support, market research, and other operations. Initial revenue streams are relatively low, capital is difficult to attract to a state-assisted institution, and state funding has generally lagged. In the autumn of 1999, the state offered funding to expand service in this area. The university recently persuaded the legislature to lift restrictions that limited efforts to serve non-traditional students. While UW institutions are now much more likely to be able to respond to these markets, demand will still probably exceed supply.

Third, institutions cannot be all things to all people. We recognize both the complexity and the opportunity in the many markets for distance education – including continuing education for alumni and others already in the workforce. Sophisticated market analysis must precede launch of new ventures. Off-campus outreach is vital to our mission as a land-grant institution, but resource limitations are a major challenge.

VIRTUAL UNIVERSITIES VERSUS TRADITIONAL EDUCATION

In contrast to the hopes of policy-makers, many in academe feared that virtual universities would lead to fast, cheap, one-size-fits-all education of suspect quality. Kenneth H. Ashworth, commissioner of the Texas Higher Education Coordinating Board, wrote in 1996 that they "could well become the model for displacing more-traditional higher education." Ashworth wrote that "the stated and implied goals of satisfying industry, bypassing faculty members, and providing mass credentialling at low cost through technology have much appeal to some politicians."[10]

Some commentators predicted that campuses would become as obsolete as medieval monasteries and that established institutions would probably not continue building on their primary campuses. As important as IT is, it is clearly not replacing the on-campus experience.

The marketplace argues against that happening. It is unlikely that significant numbers of traditional undergraduates, who actually have a choice, will choose a virtual education over more traditional institutions that are incorporating IT to improve instruction. Four factors suggest to me that most students still much prefer being on campus and will continue to do so.

First, students enjoy and appreciate the on-campus experience. In the UW system, surveys of students and alumni continue to show extremely high satisfaction – 95 per cent of students surveyed indicated satisfaction with their overall experience at UW, and 96 per cent, with their instruction. Similarly, 91 per cent of alumni said that they would attend the same institution if they could choose again, and 86 per cent, that their undergraduate education was either an exceptional or a good value.[11]

Second, life on campus is continuing to improve, with many sites focusing on building a better learning environment both in and out of the classroom. For example, Chadbourne Residential College at UW – Madison houses students who want a small liberal arts college while attending one of the world's great research universities. Chadbourne houses 650 first-year students and upperclassmen in a residence hall with a computer lab, an after-hours coffee-house, on-site academic advice, a writing assistance centre, and twenty-four-hour student services and front desk. Students and instructors share knowledge and experience and can explore connections between in- and out-of-classroom learning.

Faculty and staff members take an active role in Chadbourne, hosting discussion groups, monthly dinners, and guests-in-residence. Frequent get-togethers and field trips involve visiting scholars, writers, artists, community leaders, alumni, and others eager to share their experiences and perspectives. There are regular excursions to theatre, film, and musical events, along with a chance to talk with the artists. Students lead discussions of current events and issues of special interest to Chadbourne members. Workshops help students succeed in college and later in life: setting academic goals, studying for examinations, improving writing, finding research opportunities, competing for scholarships, finding summer internships, applying to graduate and professional school, and finding a job.

In university classrooms, curriculum offerings are evolving to take advantage of IT and to match today's requirements. Institutions have acted to ensure availability of desired courses and, if anything, to enhance a student's ability to complete a baccalaureate degree in four years. The introduction of a variety of innovations – from CD-ROMS to web-based instruction – make learning more effective and more enjoyable.

Third, while costs of studying on campus have increased, they are still generally significantly below those of virtual universities. This is a major competitive advantage for campuses, whether they are major research institutions or smaller schools focused on undergraduates.

Fourth, campuses offer a safe residential atmosphere where individuals can grow both intellectually and socially. Parents will continue to have a strong preference for having their eighteen-year-old daughters and sons in a controlled campus environment as opposed to having them live either at home or in apartments not connected to an institution. Students will continue to seek environments where they can socialize, meet mentors, and build social and professional networks.

Yet I still see significant change coming on campus. Students may not take the same number of courses from their home institution. On-line offerings make possible multi-institutional, asynchronous study. Precedent exists for accepting credits through transfer or advanced placement. For decades we have encouraged study abroad. Thus, many traditional students are already aware of alternatives.

The failure of visions of virtual universities to mature does not mean that traditional institutions need not change. Students who have been using computers since age six are now arriving on campus. To many of them, if something is not on the web, it does not exist. As the first generation to order or download music and videos from the internet, to "visit" the Louvre via a website, and to conduct electronic research directly using world-class libraries, they will have high expectations. They regard emerging IT with considerably less awe than we do. Its opportunities are a given to them. IT simply must be used to enrich instruction that has been delivered by lectures since the Middle Ages.

TECHNOLOGY TO ENHANCE
THE CAMPUS EXPERIENCE

My sense is that on-campus demands for integrating IT into the classroom for traditional students will in the near future consume most of our energy and resources. C. Peter Magrath, president of the National Association of State Universities and Land Grant Colleges (NASULGC), points out that using IT and providing distance education are not unique to private-enterprise "virtual universities." According to a survey of NASULGC members, two-thirds participate in a virtual university or employ IT to deliver distance education. Sixty-nine per cent of member institutions reported upgrading equipment for students, and 60 per cent, for the faculty and the staff. "Integrating new technology in the classroom" was one of three top IT spending priorities for 45 per cent of institutions. Members devote

5 per cent of their operating budgets to IT, with 71 per cent assessing students to help pay the cost.[12]

Some developments in the UW System demonstrate how IT is enhancing experience on campus, and one program harnesses IT to offer a degree using courses from several campuses.

Like other institutions, UW campuses are improving on-campus classrooms. For example, a faculty member in atmospheric and oceanic science at UW – Madison uses IT to reach students better, and to make his teaching more effective.[13] His students watch a web-based thunderstorm model in class. They can choose their own weather variables – temperature, dew point, pressure – to make the model thunderstorm grow or dissipate. When students repeat this exercise or variations of it outside class with interactive models on the web, they get immediate feedback on their assumptions and predictions.

Such technology also changes the traditional lecture. Note-taking services now publish classroom lectures, and class notes are posted on the web. Thus the professor uses IT to enhance classroom offerings. IT also allows students to participate in the lecture, and UW students often pair up to share information and work together on the interactive models. This occurs in class – during time when the professor used to stand in front of the room and talk to them.

CD-ROMS are improving education in fields as varied as dance and language. A professor of dance at UW – Madison developed a CD-ROM to teach students how the body moves.[14] Menu options allow them to view a particular dance movement or part of the body. In one view, a real dancer demonstrates a move, with a particular part of the body highlighted. With a mouse click, students can view the move from different angles. Another mouse click replaces the dancer with an animated skeleton that performs the same move as the real dancer. Before the advent of the CD-ROM, the professor tried to diagram these movements and concepts on a blackboard – essentially rendering a three-dimensional movement on a motionless medium, which did not always work well.

Another member of the faculty at UW – Madison developed a CD-ROM to help students learn Yorùbá – a language spoken in Nigeria. Students of Yorùbá must hear the language in order to speak it. Native speakers on the CD-ROM pronounce words in Yorùbá so that students can hear how the words should sound. When they are ready, students pronounce words into the microphone of their personal

computer. The program will play back a student's voice for comparison with the native speaker on the CD-ROM, producing a wavelength
readout of both voices to see how closely the student is matching the
native speaker's inflection.[15]

The CD-ROM allows students to "see" the language – in text and in
context. With video images, the CD-ROM demonstrates Yorùbá culture, helping students learn appropriate contexts for various words.
This is crucial for activities such as greetings. With a video image, the
student can better associate the context in which each greeting is used.

IT connects campus resources across the entire UW System. Our
Collaborative Nursing Program uses distance-education technology
to offer a bachelor of science degree in nursing to registered nurses
who have limited access to a campus that offers that degree.[16] Students choose one of five collaborating UW campuses as their "home"
institution, which provides all student-related services, the practicum,
and the capstone course that give students an integrative educational
experience.

All participating campuses offer nursing courses in the shared,
common curriculum, combining the resources of five nursing programs. Using distance technology, such as compressed video, audio-
graphics, and internet courses, students can take courses from their
home campus or anywhere in the state. The program has enrolled
increasing numbers of nursing students and received the International Teleconferencing Association's Teleconferencing Excellence
Award in 1997 for educational programming and distance learning.

IT is also transforming the very core of our institutions – libraries.
UW libraries have replaced their main frame–based electronic card
catalogues with Voyager, an integrated system for managing information.[17] Library services – such as the on-line catalogue, circulation,
and the website – have one seamless interface accessible across the
state to students and members of faculty and of staff via client–server
and Web-based technology.

Voyager supports a full range of library staff functions – such as
acquiring and cataloguing material, circulating items, and managing
reserves – allowing collections at twenty-six sites to be managed as
one collection. It expanded on-line access to audio and video material
and digital images. Materials once available to a limited readership
are now available worldwide.

UW students have vastly expanded research opportunities. From their rooms in residence, at any time of day, they can see library records, renew and recall items on-line, see up-to-the minute additions of newly acquired materials, examine course reserve material, and link themselves to full-text electronic journals and books. They can click on links within catalogue records, such as author entries and related subjects, or go directly to any site on the web for which a record includes a URL.

CONCLUSION: MORE QUESTIONS

While I am excited about each of these IT-related improvements, many questions remain – about the effects of IT on students, on institutions, and on the body of knowledge.

Students

There are indications that some students living on campus are selecting non-personal web-based instruction over classrooms. While many traditional students thrive with independent learning, others do not.

- How can we socialize students via the internet? How do we find students a real mentor on-line?
- With a virtual experience, how do we ensure that we transmit important values, such as civility?

U.S. trends project continued growth in non-traditional students (age twenty-two and older) seeking a university education. Many institutions should consider carefully whether they should address the needs of this group.

- Will distinct niches develop in higher education, with institutions selecting markets to serve based on factors that include available resources and market factors (such as pricing versus costs and, in some cases, profitability)?
- Will governments subsidize development of such programs where they see a social need, or will support have to come from the individual or his or her employer?

As more courses appear on the web, students will face vastly increased choices.

• What mechanism will emerge to guide students as consumers in selecting web-based courses? Can current accrediting bodies protect consumers?

As the amount of knowledge increases and individuals change careers, continuing education is becoming more important.

• Will IT make continuing education more accessible? Will students or their employers pay for continuing education? Or might governments offer subsidies?
• What portion of continuing education will self-paced web-based, as opposed to face-to-face, instruction provide? Will the convergence of the computer and the television shift continuing education to the home or the workplace from traditional locales?
• What will happen to students who rely on personal mentoring? Will they still finish courses when they never meet an instructor face to face?

Institutions

Just as IT will affect students' experience, it will also affect institutions.

• Will all universities embrace IT? What will be the future of those that choose not to? Will they seem unique or merely archaic?

Institutions are funding IT by raising student fees.

• Given the pressure to keep tuition affordable, how will financially challenged institutions acquire up-to-date IT?
• Can financially challenged institutions take IT into the classroom? Or will IT increase costs, forcing consolidation in instruction?
• Does IT require new talents of faculty members? If so, how will institutions help those individuals?
• Will more institutions follow the UW system, where campuses cooperate to allow students to take classes from more than one location?

- Will institutions limit students' ability to take courses from external institutions, or will they embrace a "free market"?
- Will economic status affect a student's access to an IT-based education? Will societies guarantee at least minimum access to IT in the same way that some have to medical care?

Creation and Maintenance of Knowledge

My final questions relate to how IT could affect creation, use, and maintenance of knowledge.

There are signs that students are overly reliant on web search engines for conducting research.

- Do web search engines decide what resources students use? How do we direct students to libraries as research sources?
- Will we become so enamoured of material in digital form that we will lose valuable material that it is not digitalized? Are budgets adequate to digitalize the contents of current holdings?

Advertisers and others are becoming skilled at manipulating search engines so that research results list their web pages first.

- Will researchers and authors do the same to draw attention to their own articles?
- How will IT affect language? Just as the language of aviation is English, will the web create pressure for a common language?

In the medieval church, stained glass windows conveyed messages to the illiterate.

- How will messages be conveyed to the technologically illiterate?

Verification of the accuracy of materials posted on the web is becoming difficult. Individuals who choose to liberate themselves from the peer review of a journal or the editor at a publishing house are also free from the fact-checker.

- As the volume of material available for research grows, and as significant knowledge appears in non-refereed journals, who will certify the validity of the material?

None of these questions invalidates IT. However, we must be thoughtful as we embrace it. We must make choices that strengthen institutions, students, and the cultures and societies that depend on them to transmit knowledge to future generations. With our feet planted firmly on earth, we must be visionary in adapting institutions to take advantage of the opportunities for change.

NOTES

1 Doug Bradley, "Learning Innovation Center Will Position UW System to Be a Key Educational Player in 21st Century," *University of Wisconsin System Wisconsin Ideas*; "University of Wisconsin Learning Innovations Business Plan," June 1999.
2 Goldie Blumenstyk, "Western Governors U. Takes Shape as a New Model for Higher Education," *Chronicle of Higher Education*, 6 Feb. 1998.
3 Jeffrey R. Young, "A Virtual Student Teaches Himself," *Chronicle of Higher Education*, 7 May 1999.
4 Ibid., A32, and "Passing without Distinction," *CIO Web Business*, 1 June 1999.
5 Jeffrey R. Young, "Western Governors U. Seeks $8 Million in Federal Funds," *Chronicle of Higher Education*, 28 May 1999.
6 Goldie Blumenstyk, "California Shuns 'Virtual U.,' Will Offer Own On-Line Courses," *Chronicle of Higher Education*, 11 Oct. 1998.
7 Kenneth R. Weiss, "California Virtual University Has a Collision with Reality," *Los Angeles Times*, 8 April 1999.
8 "Enrollment Figures Spur Optimism at Virtual Universities," *Chronicle of Higher Education*, 27 Nov. 1998.
9 Young, "Virtual Student."
10 Kenneth H. Ashworth, "Virtual Universities Could Produce Only Virtual Learning," *Chronicle of Higher Education*, 6 Sept. 1996.
11 University of Wisconsin System, "Accountability for Achievement: 1998 Report," Dec. 1998.
12 National Association of State Universities and Land Grant Colleges, "Public Research Universities Active Participants in 'Virtual Universities,' As Information Technology Affects Nearly Every Area of Campus," news release, 28 May 1999.
13 Steve Ackerman, "Teaching and Learning with Technology: Progress and Prospects," Madison, 27–28 May 1999.

14 Buff Brennan, "Teaching and Learning with Technology: Progress and Prospects," Madison, 27–28 May 1999.

15 Antonia Schleicher, "Teaching and Learning with Technology: Progress and Prospects," Madison, 27–28 May 1999.

16 UW – Extension web page, www.uwex.edu, and UW – Green Bay web page, www.uwgb.edu.

17 UW – Madison Library web page, www.library.wisc.edu; Office of News and Affairs, UW – Madison, "Campus Libraries Plan Electronic Catalog Upgrade," 28 April 1999; and Anita Clark, "UW Libraries Switching to New Electronic Catalog," *Wisconsin State Journal*, 1 June 1999.